AN EASY GUIDE TO REACHING MUSLIMS

WILLIAM E. MASIH

How to Reach
MUSLIMS

Go & Save

MINISTRIES

COMMENDATIONS

"This is a very helpful and practical book on an important subject, i.e., sharing the Gospel of Jesus with our Muslim friends. Having been instructed on how to share the Christian faith with others, it is very easy for us to pursue this on a 'one size fits all' basis. The author gently corrects this approach by showing us that it is best to start from the Quran rather than the Bible. It reminds us that Jesus 'takes us as we are' - as we are, not where others would initially like us to be. The testimonies and personal experiences which William Masih shares with us make the subject real rather than merely theoretical. An excellent touch! I am sure this book will be of real benefit to all who read it and be used as a source of reference, especially in the matter of 'do's' and 'don'ts'. It is a pleasure and honour to commend it to you."

Rod Langston
Deputy Chairman of Ebenezer
Operation Exodus UK and former Church Pastor

"It is a really excellent book and I pray that it will be much used by the Lord to bring Muslims to Christ but to also encourage believers to share the gospel with them in an acceptable way. There are many books about how to evangelise to Muslims but here William Masih brings us his unique personal experience. This book helpfully explains the way through using the Quran to reach the Muslim mind and culture. May it be widely read and may many find Christ as a result."

Jill Southern
Ellel Ministries International, Executive Leader;
Regional Director of S.E Asia and China

3

"Many Christians are fearful of sharing their faith with Muslims because of a lack of knowledge and understanding. William Masih has done an excellent job in giving us this book. It is concise, accessible and yet thorough enough to give the reader confidence in sharing the truth of Jesus with their Muslim neighbours and friends. William's passion and deep love for the Muslim people comes through his writing. I wholeheartedly recommend this book."

Steve Uppal
Senior Pastor of All Nations Church, Wolverhampton

"William Masih is an experienced minister, author and a church planter, who has experienced life-threatening persecution for his faith in Jesus. After an amazing encounter with Jesus many years ago, he is clearly called to help us to understand and reach our Muslim friends with the glorious Gospel of Jesus Christ. This book is full of testimonies and excellent instructions that will help every Christian to understand and reach out to Muslims effectively."

Ian Christensen
Senior Pastor of NLCCi
and Principal of New Life Bible School

"If you are not sure how to lovingly but truthfully win the hearts and minds of Muslims for the gospel – William's very instructive and highly informed book will be an answer to prayer."

Gerald Coates
Pioneer, speaker, author and broadcaster

ACKNOWLEDGEMENTS

My deepest appreciation to...

Most important, my sincere gratitude to Jesus, my Lord and brother. How can words adequately acknowledge all you have done for me. I love you more than I am able to express.

To my wife Darkhshinda for being the most faithful supporter, wife, and mother of our children. To our three daughters Naysa, Remelia and Nathania. Each of you have brought tremendous joy to my life and are special treasures. To Sajjad Ahmed, Daniel Lopez-Ferreiro and Ash Kotecha for the love, kindness, and wisdom you have selflessly given has touched and strengthened my heart. I thank God for your friendship and support. To Esther Kotecha and Sandra Sinclair for your unwavering support and faithfulness and for your designing and editing skills in this project.

CONTENTS

DEDICATION

I dedicate this book to all the believers
of the world who have been persecuted or are
being persecuted in Muslim countries because
of their faith in the Lord Jesus Christ.

INTRODUCTION

I never intended to write a book. It began simply as I started answering the questions that Muslims put to me.

More than twenty years ago, I began to share my faith with Muslims. I soon learnt something that has stuck with me through the years: evangelism is more of a process than an event. Evangelism usually involves a process over time and takes a lot of prayer, persistence and divine guidance.

I have realised that many people want to reach out to Muslims but do not know how to do it. When a Muslim asks a Christian a question regarding the Christian faith, Christians often open the Bible and start giving them references and quotes. Most Christians are ignorant to the fact that Muslims do not believe in the Bible as a reliable account. They believe it is corrupt. So whatever we Christians tell them, they do not believe. That is the reason why many Christians have failed in the Muslim world. However, when we approach it from the perspective of the Quran they then understand it and believe it but if we talk to them from the Bible's perspective then they will not believe it. Many Christians are scared of Muslims and many do not know how to answer their questions.

Remember, Muslims are not far away from us - overseas, living in mountains or hidden in the desert. There is no need to prepare for years before you go to them in their own countries, where you would be ignorant of their social, educational and traditional life and, then come back after years empty-handed, disappointed and rejected. Muslims are here today on your streets; they are your neighbours, at your schools, universities, workplaces and, sitting next to you on the bus or at the park.

God is bringing Muslims out from the place of bondage and darkness where they can now hear and accept the Word of God. God is bringing them into a place of freedom and light where they can hear the gospel, believe it freely, and follow it without any fear.

Remember: darkness cannot take over the light but light can take over the darkness. You do not need to spend a lot of money to go to them; God is bringing them to you. ALL you need is to be brave and share the gospel with them. So, be patient and strong because Muslims have a distorted image of Christianity.

I was born and brought up in a Muslim country. I studied Islam for sixteen years as a compulsory subject and then later, I studied for a Master's degree in Islamic Studies.

The purpose of this book is to equip believers and encourage them to engage in Muslim evangelism. This book will help you to know Islam better, and you will be equipped to answer questions from Muslims according to their Islamic perspective.

Many people come and ask my views about the growth of Islam. It is true that Islam is growing in Europe, but not the way it is presented. Islam is increasing by birth and by immigration only; the conversion rate is very low. There are so many Afghani, Pakistani, Kashmiri, Iranian, Iraqi, Syrian, Lebanese, Kurdish, Somali, Nigerian, South Sudanese, Palestinian, Bangladeshi, Moroccan and Kosovo refugees in Europe and the number of these people is growing day by day.

In terms of the Muslim population, there are:

- 1.8 billion in the world.
- 307 million in Africa.
- 778 million in Asia.
- 35 million in Europe.
- 1.4 million in Latin America

...as of 2015 according to a Pew Research Centre estimate.

By this time tomorrow, thirty-five thousand Muslims will die without knowing Christ.

Number of refugees received, by country (end 2017 - UNHCR:)

Germany 1,413,127	*France 401,729*	*Italy 354,698*
Sweden 327,709	*Latvia 234,296*	*Austria 172,570*
UK 162,299	*Netherlands 111,629*	*Estonia 80,769*
Spain 54,028	*Denmark 47,927*	*Finland 26,704*
Poland 25,965	*Bulgaria 21,956*	*Ireland 12,539*
Malta 9,389	*Hungary 6,508*	*Czech Republic 5,957*
Romania 5,702	*Lithuania 5,029*	*Luxembourg 3,624*
Slovakia 2,480	*Portugal 1682*	*Slovenia 892*

CHAPTER 1

What is Christianity according to Islam?

I was born into a Roman Catholic family in Punjab, Pakistan. I gave my life to Jesus when I was 17 years old and since that time I have been walking with Jesus. My childhood was mediocre. It was not very good and I was not a particularly well behaved student. I spent most of my time outside with my friends, wandering around the streets. All my friends were drug addicts and one of my friends actually died because of heavy drugs use. I was in a gang and we use to fight rival gangs. Although a gang member, I did not approve of all what they were doing. I had a deep hunger for God and I wanted to know the true living God but did not know how to know Him and follow Him. So my life was miserable and I was not content at all. I had no peace and did not know the purpose of my life. I used to tell myself that I will die one day without achieving anything in life. For me, my life was meaningless. I used to think that maybe one day I will also start taking drugs and will die an addict. I am very thankful to God that He picked me from that dirty pit. If Jesus did not pick me from there, maybe now at this time, I might also be a drug user, taking drugs with my friends, in any corner of Islamabad, or maybe in jail with the gang I was an active part of.

When I finished high school, I studied different religions like: Hinduism, Sikhism, Baha'ism, New Age, Mormonism, Jehovah Witness, Islam and Buddhism. I did not study all these religions at home but I would actively go to their place of worship: studying Islam I visited the mosque; for Hinduism it was a visit to the Hindu Temple; for Sikhism a visit to the Sikh temple and for Baha'ism I would go to the Baha Centre. My overall conclusion, i.e. my exhaustive research and visits, was that God simply did not exist. When I went to college, I met a Christian friend who tried to evangelise to me and I told him my overall conclusion:

"There is no God!"

He was persistent and added, "No, there is one true living God. All the other religions teach you how you can reach out to God but only Christianity tells you how God can reach out to you."

Each time we met, he reiterated:

"There is a true living God and you can see Him. Our God is not like other gods of this world. If you want to see Him, He will come and will talk to you."

So I told him, "If I can see Him or observe Him then He is not God."

He was relentless. Each time we met he echoed that the God of Christianity can be seen. So one day I said to him that I wanted to challenge His God; whoever He is, I wanted to see him. I concluded, "Your God has 30 days. Within 30 days I want to see Him." Delighted and confident, he affirmed that surely His God will come and talk to me during that time.

He told me that every night before I go to bed that I was to pray. He told me to be very sincere and pray the following from my heart: "God, the creator of this universe, a true living God whoever you are come and show me your face I want to see you." He then confirmed, confidently,

"He will come and will talk to you."

My response was, "That is so easy; I will do it!" So I prayed for 29

nights and nobody came. I use to tell my friends,
"See, there is no God."

However, something happened! On the 30th night, when I was sleeping, I heard a voice from outside.

"William! William!"

Someone was calling my name. I went out to the kitchen side of the court yard but nobody was present. I was afraid and came back and slept again. After some time, I heard that same voice which was calling me:

"William! William!"

I ran outside but still there was no one there. I returned to my bedroom. Standing in the kitchen door, words came into my mind and at that time I did not know that these words were already written in the Bible. I responded,

"Here I am God, what do you want to show or tell me?" As I said those words, I saw a man in a white robe that came to the roof. (In my country roofs are flat and not triangular as they are in Europe and there were stairs coming down from the roof).
The man walked down the stairs and stood in front of me and asked me,

"Will you allow me to come into your bedroom?"

I did not say anything. I just walked back to my bedroom and sat at the head of the bed. He came in and sat at the foot of the bed. While He was sitting on the bed he told me that He was Jesus. I did not believe Him. I said to the man:

"Okay, if you are Jesus then my brother and sister-in-law are sleeping in that room (pointing towards their door) go and bring them here."

So the man went and bought my brother and sister-in-law into the room. I was sitting at the head of my bed and my brother and sister-in-law came and sat on the other side of the bed and the man who said that he is Jesus sat at the same place as my feet. Then all four of us prayed together.

After praying my brother and sister-in-law went back to their room and after some time the man later left.

The next morning, my sister-in-law came to me and enquired if I had had a nightmare the previous night. I replied that I did not. She told me that she and her husband came to my room and witnessed me praying and crying.

I asked her, "Did you pray with me?"

She responded, "No."

I asked the man if He could bring my sister-in-law and my brother to me, which He did. They had not prayed with me but when they came and saw me they then went back. I believe that when they came their spirits stayed and prayed with us but their physical bodies left.

Then I asked her, "Did you see someone else in my room?"

"No," she replied and added, "You were alone praying and crying." When I testified to her that Jesus visited me and I saw Jesus, she said that they could feel the presence of God in my room. That was the day when my life changed completely. After that day, I threw away all the books I had of different religions and since that day I confessed Jesus as my Lord and saviour. Now, the Bible is the only book I love and read.

Since that day I have experienced many highs and lows in my life but Jesus has never ever left me alone. He is forever with me in all kind of circumstances because He has promised; "I will never leave you nor forsake you." He is always with me.

Islam has a completely different view about Christianity. The writer of the Quran has very little knowledge of the Bible. Christianity is not based on the teachings of Christ but on Christ Himself. If you remove Christ from Christianity then it will collapse, because Christ is the foundation of Christianity. Christ is the pillar of Christianity. Christianity stands on the sacrificial death of Christ; He took all the sins of this world and restored the broken relationship between man and God.

All the religions of the world are based on the teachings of their founders: Islam is based on the teachings of Muhammad, not on Muhammad; Sikhism is based on the teachings of Guru Nanak but not on Guru Nanak and Buddhism is based on the teachings of Buddha but not on Buddha. Muhammad is seen as the 'seal of the prophets' - the last and the greatest. However, he is not seen as more than a man.

There are some common misconceptions about the Christian faith held by Muslims. If you want to work among Muslims then it is very important that you know what Muslims believe about Christianity.

1) Muslims perceive Christianity to be based on the teachings of Paul, not Jesus.

Molana Muhammad Tariq Usmani has written a book entitled, 'What is Christianity?' In this book, he writes:

"It is true that Hazrat Isa was born in Bani Israel and he teaches them about Allah and his commandments. But after deep research and investigations, it has been revealed that the teaching of Hazrat Isa was soon after his ascension are corrupted. The teachings and sayings of Isa were replaced with traditions and customs. These traditions and customs have been shaped into Christianity. Now we have concluded that the founder of Christianity is not Isa but Paul." [1]

However, in all the epistles of Paul, or Peter or John or James, there is no new commandment or law introduced. The epistles merely explain the teachings of Jesus Christ. Further, Christianity is not a religion but a relationship. On account of this relationship, we are born into the family of God and we call God 'Abba [Father]'. Because of this relationship, we become brothers and sisters of

Christ and co-heirs with Him of eternal life in the Presence of God the Father.

2) Dr Ansari, has written in his book 'Islam and Christianity in the Modern World':

"In Christianity the first sin of Adam and Eve was forgiven that's why now every child who is born in this world is holy and pure. Sin does not transfer from one generation to another generation." [2]

However, Christian doctrine states that every child who has been born in this world is born with a sinful nature and is a natural sinner:

- Psalm 51:5 says: *"Behold, I was shaped in iniquity; and in sin did my mother conceive me."*
- Romans 3:10 says: *"There is no one righteous, not even one."*
- Romans 3:23 says: *"For all have sinned and fall short of the glory of God."*

3) Muslims perceive the Trinity to include Mary, the mother of Christ:

"The followers of Christianity believe in the trinity and they say that God, (the) Son and Holy Mary are three persons but one God." [3]

However, the Christian concept of the Trinity is something entirely different. According to the Christian faith, the Trinity is: God the Father, God the Son and God the Holy Spirit, three Persons but one Being. Mary the mother of Christ is not part of the Trinity.

4) In Christianity, the followers of Jesus believe that God is

their Father. Hazrat Isa did not teach the people that Allah is his Father and his followers can call God "Abba." Rather it is taught that the followers of Isa were deceived by Paul and he introduced them to this theology later:

Quran 5:18 says:
"But the Jews and Christians say, 'we are the children of Allah and His beloved.' then why does he punish you for your sins? Rather, you are human beings from among those he has created."

However, in Christianity, God has revealed Himself as a Father:

John 1:12-13 says:
"Yet to all who received Him, to those who believed in His Name, He gave the right to become children of God; children born not of natural descent, nor of human decision or a husband's will, but born of God."

Even Jesus himself taught his disciples that when they pray, they should call God their Father: Matthew 6:9 says: *"Our Father in heaven…"*

5) Christians - followers of Jesus - believe that Jesus was crucified, died on the cross and on the third day He was raised from the dead.

"The founder of Christianity, Hazrat Isa didn't die on the cross, even he was not raised from the dead and nor did people see him after resurrection." [4]

As Christians we say that Jesus revealed Himself to his disciples and other people during a period of forty days. Then, in front of his disciples He ascended into heaven. He will come back again to judge the whole world.

After reading all these comparisons, it is easy to see that Christianity, according to Islam, is not what Christians believe and practice. According to Islam, Isa is not the person Christians believe and follow. Hazrat Maryam, the mother of Isa, is a completely different woman from the Mary who is the mother of Jesus.

Endnotes:

1. Molana Muhammad Tariq Usmani, *'What is Christianity?'* Dawat Academy, international Islamic University, Islamabad, page 75.

2. Dr Ansari F.R, *'Islam and Christianity in the Modern World,'* The World Federation of Islamic Mission Islamic Centre, B Block, North Nazimabad, Karachi-33, Pakistan, page 6.

3. Molana Muhammad Tariq Usmani, *'What is Christianity?'* Dawat Academy, international Islamic University, Islamabad, page 16.

4. Maqsood Ayaz, *'Muhammad Nasir People's Encyclopaedia,'* Anar Kali Lahore, page 507, column 1.

1.1 *Different God: Allah and Yahweh*

Allah is the word for god in Arabic. But does that mean that when Muslims and Christians pray, we are praying to the same God?

No.

Why? Because the character or description of Allah, in the Quran, and the character or description of Yahweh, in the Bible, are not the same. Let me state it another way: the content of the word 'Allah' to Muslims who believe the Quran, and the content of the word 'Yahweh' to Christians who believe the Bible, are not the same at all. The Quranic revelation of Allah and the Biblical revelation of Yahweh are in profound conflict. Many Arabic speaking Christians and intellectually honest followers of Islam say that they are two different gods.

Arabic speaking Christians say that they should not use the term Allah to describe God and the Arabic bible should not use Allah to describe God. Many intellectually honest Muslims say that Yahweh (God) and Allah are not the same because the Quran specifically teaches that Allah has no son. Faithful Muslims will never say that they pray to Yahweh God or they want any revelation from Yahweh because to them Jesus and The Holy Spirit are not a part of the Godhead. According to them, Christians believe in three Gods and Yahweh is not a singular deity. The same god could not give two opposing revelations of Himself. When you consider that both the Bible and Quran contradict each other, one is left with only two possible conclusions:

(1) Either one is true and the other is false or
(2) Both are false.

However, it is irrational to suggest that one who is truly God would give two separate revelations that contradict each other. It is very difficult to say that both are false. Definitely one is true and the other is false. Or if both are true, they are certainly not speaking of the same god.

Christians who blindly say: "After all, we both serve the same god, we just call him by different names," they must decide which God do they believe. Simply stated, Yahweh, the God of Christianity, and Allah, the God of Islam are not the same. The United States President, Donald Trump visited Israel, and the Israeli president in his welcome speech stated: "Christians, Muslims and Jews worship the same God." Did you hear that? Do you agree with the Israeli President's statement? I do not agree with him. The Quran supports the Israeli president's words:

Quran 29:46 says:

"Do not agree with the people of the Scripture (Jews and Christians) except in the nicest possible manner - unless they transgress and say "we believe in what was revealed to us, and in what was revealed to you and our God and your God is one and the same; to him we are supporters."

Allah and Yahweh are in complete contrast to one another. Let me give you a brief comparison:

YAHWEH: The Bible clearly states that God is love and He does not hate anyone:

John 3:16: *"God loved the sinful world."*
Romans 5:8: *"God has proved his love for sinners in this matter that Christ died for the sinners."*
Ezekiel 18:23: *"God hates sin but loves the sinners."*

ALLAH: The Quran teaches that Allah loves those he chooses to love and hates those he chooses to hate. According to the Quranic teachings, Allah's love or hate is in response to human behaviour.

3:140: *"Allah loves not those that do wrong."*
2:190: *"Allah hates the transgressors."*
2:276: *"Allah hates ungrateful and wicked creatures."*
3:32, 30:45: *"Allah hates those who reject faith."*

YAHWEH: Yahweh is merciful and compassionate towards sinners.
ALLAH: Allah is not merciful towards sinners.

YAHWEH: Yahweh is more gracious than judgmental.
ALLAH: Allah is more judgmental than gracious.

YAHWEH: Yahweh is close, personal and invites us to approach His throne of glory.

ALLAH: Allah is distant, unknowable and unapproachable.

YAHWEH: Yahweh has revealed Himself as well as His will. John 17:3 *"This is eternal life that they may know you, the only true God and the one you have sent - Jesus Christ."*
ALLAH: Allah reveals His will but not Himself.

YAHWEH: Yahweh is everywhere even in the bathroom and your bedroom. He is omnipresent.
ALLAH: Allah is not everywhere. According to the Quran and Islamic teachings, Allah is not in the bathroom. He lives in heaven above.

YAHWEH: Yahweh is Father to every single person who receives Christ as His Lord and Saviour. Yahweh has a personal relationship with human beings. Yahweh is not a grandfather of anyone. He is the Father of mankind.
ALLAH: Allah has no son and he does not have any personal relationship with human beings.

YAHWEH: Yahweh loves us so much that he sent his son Jesus Christ to die for our sins. This was determined in eternity past, before even you and I were born and, before any of mankind had fallen into sin.
ALLAH: The Quran teaches that there is no need for Allah to provide a sacrifice for sin. Even Jesus did not die on the Cross as a sacrificial Lamb.

YAHWEH: Yahweh has revealed Himself as Father, Son and Holy Spirit.
ALLAH: Allah exists as a singular unity that has no 'partners.'

YAHWEH: Yahweh has revealed Himself as a Father. Father of Jesus and us all.

ALLAH: Allah has 99 names in the Quran but father is not one of them. In Islam it is blasphemy to call God 'Father.'

YAHWEH: Yahweh has spoken to people throughout history and continues to do so today.
ALLAH: Allah has never spoken directly to Muhammad or any of His followers or any other person in history.

Allah has denied: the Trinity; the Fatherhood of God; the Sonship of Jesus Christ; the deity of the Holy Spirit; the crucifixion and the resurrection of Jesus Christ; but Yahweh has not.

1.2 *Different Jesus: Isa or Jesus*

Isa, is the name used in the Quran for Jesus, which was introduced to Muhammad by some anti-Christians. The root of this name is Esau, the twin brother of Jacob, who was outcast from the promise of God.

Every single Muslim will say that they believe in Isa. Unless he believes in Isa, he cannot be a true Muslim. But their Quaranic understanding of Isa is completely different. They believe that Isa is just a prophet of Allah and Allah gave him power to perform miracles. He is just like other prophets but with some extra power to perform miracles. Isa of the Quran and Jesus of the Bible are not the same. When you study the life, birth, teachings, miracles and claims of Isa and Jesus thoroughly, it is clear that they are actually describing two different people entirely. There is a vast difference in their personalities, births, teachings, miracles and the way they lived their lives for it to be safely concluded that they are not the same person. Isa, of the Quran, and Jesus, of the Bible, are two different people. Here I want to present to you a comparison of the life, birth, teachings, miracles and claims of Jesus and of Isa, and then I will leave the decision to you whether they are two different people or two names of the one person.

JESUS: An Angel informed Mary she is to call her son Jesus.

Luke 1:31-32 says,
"You will conceive and give birth to a son and you are to call him Jesus. He will be great and will be called the son of the most high. The Lord God will give him the throne of his father David."

ISA: According to the Quran, Jesus' real name is Isa. Hamidullah Muhammad writes in his book called 'Islam and Christianity' page 19 that *"Isa is the real name of Jesus but later on his disciples gave him a new name, Jesus"*.

JESUS: Virgin born and conceived by the Holy Spirit.
ISA: Virgin born; He was created in the womb of Mary by Allah. Isa is a similar creation to Adam. (Quran 3:59, 19:20-22, 21:91)

JESUS: Born in a stable and laid in a manger. (Luke 2:7)
ISA: Born under a palm tree. *"And the pain of childbirth drove her to the trunk of a palm tree."* (Quran 19:22)

JESUS: Never said that He had brought a book and never spoke in the cradle as a child.
ISA: Came with a book at the time of his birth. He told the Jews even when he could not speak.

"So she pointed to him. They said, "How can we speak to one who is in the cradle a child? He said, indeed I am the servant of Allah. He has given me the scripture and made me a prophet." (Quran 19:29-30)

JESUS: Son of God. (Matthew 3:17, John 10:30).
ISA: Called son of Mary. Allah is not a Father and has no son and daughter; to say so is 'Shirk', which means an unforgivable sin.

JESUS: 30 years old when he started His ministry.
"Now Jesus himself was about thirty years old when he began his ministry." (Luke 3:23.)
ISA: He was 35 years old when he started his public ministry according to Mrs. Ulfat Aziz in her book 'Islam and Christianity' page 11.

JESUS: Eternal, co-equal and co-eternal with the Father and Holy Spirit. (John 8:58, 17:5, 1:1-14, Colossians 1:15-29, Philippians 2:5-11, Hebrews 1:1-13).
ISA: Created from the dust as Adam was (Quran 3:59). Isa is only a man and a prophet.

JESUS: 33 and half years old when he was crucified.
ISA: Muhammad told Aisha that Isa, son of Mary, was 120 years old when he was taken to heaven and Muhammad believed he would die when he will be 60 years old.

JESUS: The mediator between God and man (1 Timothy 2:5). Jesus died on the cross for our sins. (1 Corinthians 15:3, 2 Corinthians 5:21)
ISA: Not a mediator between Allah and man.

JESUS: Christ's finished Work on the Cross provides forgiveness of sins and eternal life by God's grace through faith.
ISA: Did not die on the cross. Views within Islam differ as to who died on the cross:

- Isa hid himself while one of his disciples died in his place;
- Allah made Judas Iscariot to look like Jesus and take his place;

- Simon of Cyrene took Jesus' place.
- Allah would never let his prophet die in such a way. Forgiveness of sins and eternal life are achieved by submitting to Allah and performing good deeds; atonement is not needed. (Quran 11:114, 17:15, 35:18)

JESUS: Rose from the dead and ascended into heaven after his resurrection and now seated at the right hand of the Father.
ISA: Did not die and did not rise from the dead. Allah called Isa into heaven.

JESUS: Will return physically and visibly one day to establish his earthly kingdom.
ISA: Will return one day to proclaim Islam and establish Islam on earth. Isa will defeat the antichrist, kill all pigs, break all crosses, and He will die and be buried beside Muhammad.

JESUS: Will return in glory. He said, *"I am the living one; I was dead, and now look, I am alive forever and ever! And I hold the keys of death and Hades."* (Revelation 1:18).
ISA: Jesus will come again, marry and will have children. After living for 40 years He will die. (People's encyclopedia, p507). He will be buried in Muhammad's tomb and will resurrect on the Day of Judgment with Muhammad.

JESUS: Has authority to forgive sins. Jesus said, all authority in heaven and on earth has been given to me.
ISA: Cannot forgive sins and does not claim to have any authority over heaven and earth.

JESUS: He is at the right hand of God and is interceding for us. (Romans 8:34).
ISA: Will never intercede for anyone.

JESUS: Will judge the whole world.
ISA: Has no power to judge the world.

JESUS: Proved His authority over nature by walking on water and calming the storm.
ISA: Had no authority over nature.

JESUS: He said that wherever two or three people are gathered together in MY Name, I am in the midst of them.
ISA: Not present everywhere at the same time.

JESUS: He said, *"I and the Father are one."* (John 10:30) His hearers understood that meant He was claiming authority with God in heaven.
ISA: Not equal to God.

JESUS: Through Him all things were made; without him nothing was made that has been made.
ISA: Nothing was created by or through him.

1.3 *Different Mary: Mary or Maryam?*

In the Quran the mother of Jesus is called Hazrat Maryam. She is the holiest woman in the Quran. There is one whole chapter devoted to her in the Quran.

When we look into the lives of Mary and Hazrat Maryam, it becomes clear that these are not two names of the same person. Here, I want to give you a brief comparison of these two characters:

HAZRAT MARYAM: Parents names are Hazrat Emraan (Father) and Hannah (Mother).

MARY: Parents thought to be Joachim and Anne.

HAZRAT MARYAM: A Nazirite, dedicated to God from the womb: When, Hannah, in her old age, was expecting a child, with the birth of a son in mind, she made an oath to Allah that the child to be born would be free from all worldly affairs especially dedicated to Allah's service. Allah blessed her with a daughter, who was to be the mother of Isa.

"When the wife of Emraan said, "My Lord, indeed I have pledged to you what is in my womb, consecrated (for your service). So accept this from me." (Quran 3:35)

MARY: Not a Nazirite, dedicated to God from the womb in the Bible.

HAZRAT MARYAM: Special provision from Allah:

"Every time Zechariah entered upon her in the prayer chamber, he found with her provision. He said,"O Maryam, from where is this (coming) to you?" She said, "It is from Allah. Indeed, Allah provides for whom he will without account." (Quran 3:37)

MARY: Did not receive any supernatural provision in the Bible.

HAZRAT MARYAM: Hazrat Maryam was assigned to the care of Zakariyya (the father of John the Baptist) and Zakariyya was the chosen guardian for her. He disciples her while she was in the service of Allah:

"So the Lord accepted her with good acceptance and caused her to grow in a good manner and put her in the care of Zakariyya." (Quran 3:37)

MARY: But Mary was not a disciple and looked after by Zakariyya who was the father of John the Baptist.

HAZRAT MARYAM: Hazrat Maryam was the sister of Aaron and Moses. She was from the tribe of Aaron.

"O sister of Aaron, your father was not a man of evil, nor was your

31

mother unchaste." (Quran 19:28)

MARY: But Mary was not the sister of Aaron and Moses. There is thousands of years between Aaron, Moses and Mary the mother of Jesus. Aaron and Moses had one sister called Maryam but she was not the mother of Jesus.

HAZRAT MARYAM: Hazrat Maryam withdrew herself to a far remote place.
"So she conceived him and she withdrew with him to a remote place." (Quran 19:22)

MARY: But Mary didn't live in isolation in any remote place. There is only one occasion in the gospels when Mary went to visit her cousin Elizabeth and her husband Zechariah just for three months and after three months she came back.

HAZRAT MARYAM: Hazrat Maryam before she conceived, an angel came to her as a well-proportioned man.
"And she took, in seclusion from them, a screen. Then we sent to her our angel, and he represented himself to her as a well-proportioned man." (Quran 19:17)

In another translation it says:
"Then she put a screen away from them, then we sent our spiritual towards her and he appeared before her in the shape of a healthy man."

There are different interpretations of this verse in different sects of Islam. One group says that an angel had sex with Maryam and that is the way her son was born. Many Muslims say that because he was born without a human father that is why some Christians call Isa the son of God.

MARY: However, the Bible does not say that an angel came to Mary as a healthy man.

HAZRAT MARYAM: When an angel came to Hazrat Maryam,

32

he said to her that Allah has sent me to you that I give you a pure son. *"He said, I am only a messenger of your Lord. Allah has sent me to you that I may give you a pure son."* (Quran 19:19)

But when an angel came to Mary, he said to her, *"Greetings, you who are highly favoured! The Lord is with you. Don't be afraid, Mary; you have found favour with God. You will conceive and give birth to a son, and you are to call him Jesus. He will be great and will be called the Son of the Most High God. The Lord God will give him the throne of his father David,"* (Luke 1:28-33) *"and he will reign over Jacob's descendants forever; his kingdom will never end."*

MARY: Remember! The Quran states that she was given a son and the Bible says that Mary was highly favoured.

HAZRAT MARYAM: Hazrat Maryam cursed herself and wanted to die before the birth of her child.
"And the pains of child birth drove her to the trunk of a palm tree. She said, Oh, I wish I had died before this and was in oblivion forgotten." (Quran 19:23)
MARY: But Mary didn't wish to die. She was happy and she rejoiced and worshiped God with a song.
"And Mary said, My soul glorifies the Lord and my spirit rejoices in God my saviour, for He has been mindful of the humble state of His servant. From now on all generations will call me blessed; for the Mighty One has done great things for me holy is His name." (Luke 1:46-49)

HAZRAT MARYAM: Hazrat Maryam gave birth to her son Isa under the palm tree in a far remote area where nobody was around her. *"And the pains of child birth drove her to the trunk of a palm tree."* (Quran 19:23)
MARY: But Mary gave birth to her son in a manger in Bethlehem.
"And she gave birth to her firstborn, a son. She wrapped him in clothes and placed him in a manger, because there was no guest room available for them." (Luke 2:7)

HAZRAT MARYAM: Hazrat Maryam was disgraced by the people when she gave birth to her son and they said to her that you have done a thing unprecedented.

"Then she brought him to the people, carrying him. They said, O Maryam, you have certainly done a thing unprecedented." (Quran 19:27)

MARY: *But When Mary gave birth to her son Jesus. A great company of the heavenly host appeared with the angel, praising God. When the angels had left them and gone into heaven, the shepherds hurried off and found Mary, Joseph and the baby, who was lying in the manger. The shepherds returned glorifying and praising God for all the things they had heard and seen. The kings bowed down before him and presented him expensive gifts."* (Luke 2:8-20) Nobody disgraced her or cursed her.

HAZRAT MARYAM: Hazrat Maryam spoke a lie as Allah had instructed her to do so.

"So eat and drink, and cool your eye. And if you see any man, say, I have vowed a fast to the gracious God; I will therefore not speak this day to any human being." (Quran 19:26)

MARY: But Mary the mother of Jesus did not speak any lie.

HAZRAT MARYAM: Hazrat Maryam took Isa to Galilee with herself because of the disgrace and insults she faced.[5]

MARY: But Mary did not take her child to Galilee because of the disgrace and insults she faced. The Bible says in Luke 2:39:

"When Joseph and Mary had done everything required by the law of the Lord, they returned to Galilee to their own town of Nazareth."

Endnotes:

5. People's Insiclopedia, Maqsood Ayaz and Muhammad Nasir, Chocke Anar Kali, Lahore. Page 506 and column 2.

1.4 Different Books: Bible or Quran?

The Bible is divided into two major sections as the Old Testament and the New Testament. In the Old Testament, the New Testament is concealed but in the New Testament, the Old Testament is revealed. There are 66 books in the Bible. The Old Testament consists of 39 books while the New Testament consists of 27 books. The first five books of the Old Testament are called the Torah, also known as the **Penateuch**. They are *Genesis, Exodus, Leviticus, Numbers and Deuteronomy*.

There are historical books, namely: *Joshua, Judges, Ruth, 1 Samuel, 2 Samuel, 1 Kings, 2 Kings, 1 Chronicles, 2 Chronicles, Ezra, Nehemiah, and Esther.*

The poetry books are: *Job, Psalms, Proverbs, Ecclesiastes, and Song of Solomon.*

The books of the Prophets are divided into two parts, the Major Prophets and the Minor Prophets. All the Prophets are the same but the books are divided according to their sizes because some books are big and some are small.

The Major Prophets are:
Isaiah, Jeremiah, Lamentations, Ezekiel and Daniel.

The Minor Prophets are:
Hosea, Joel, Amos, Obadiah, Jonah, Micah, Nahum, Habakkuk, Zephaniah, Haggai, Zechariah, and Malachi.

The New Testament:
The first four books of the New Testament are called the

Gospels, named after the writers, (who had been with Jesus) *Matthew, Mark, Luke and John.*

The history of the early Church is called the Acts of the Apostles and is as follows:

The Epistles:
These are letters which are divided into two parts, Pauline Epistles and General Epistles.
- The Pauline Epistles: These are the letters written by Paul to the specified Churches, namely: *Romans, 1 Corinthians, 2 Corinthians, Galatians, Ephesians, Philippines, Colossians, 1 Thessalonians, 2 Thessalonians, 1 Timothy, 2 Timothy, Titus* and *Philemon.*
- General Epistles: This is one letter written to the Jewish Christians in general, namely: *Hebrews* and the seven letters written to Christians generally named after the writers: *James, 1 Peter, 2 Peter, 1 John, 2 John, 3 John* and *Jude.*

The book of the End Times:
This is the last book of the Bible in the New Testament known as the book of *Revelation.*

All these books are similar to each other and there is no contradiction. Their message, history, names of people, life stories and the prophets are not only the same but consistent. However, in contrast if you read the Quran, you will quickly conclude that it differs significantly from the Bible with regards to the various events, history, life stories of the people and, the names of the Prophets. You will notice that many of the prophets from the Quran are not mentioned in either the Old or the New Testament books. Here are some differences:

In the Quran, one of Noah's sons separated himself from the rest of the family and died in the flood waters. After the flood, the ark came to rest on Mount Judi in the Anatolian range of modern

Turkey. (Quran 11:32-48).

In the Bible, all members of Noah's family were saved from the flood and the ark came to rest on Mount Ararat in the Armenian Highlands of Turkey. (Genesis 7:1-13, 8:4).

In the Quran, Abraham dwelt in a valley without cultivation by the Kabah. (Quran 14:37) a valley thought to have been the valley of Mecca.

In the Bible, Abraham dwelt in Hebron, nineteen miles south of modern Jerusalem. (Genesis 13:18).

In the Quran, Abraham offered Ishmael as a sacrifice to God. (Quran 37:99-109).

In the Bible, Abraham offered Isaac as a sacrifice to God. (Genesis 22:1-13)

In the Quran, Abraham destroyed his father's idols at night time and in the morning he refused to destroy the idols. He encouraged the people to ask from the idols who destroyed them. He told the people that these idols were not able to protect themselves. (Quran 21:51-59)

In the Bible, Abraham did not destroy his father's idols but Gideon destroyed his father's idols. (Judges 6:25-32)

In the Quran, Abraham was thrown into the fire and he was in the fire for three days and God cooled the fire down and protected him. (Quran 21:68-70)

In the Bible, Abraham was not thrown into the fire but Shadrach, Meshach and Abednego were thrown into the fire and God saved them in the fire. (Daniel 3:19-25).

In the Quran, the wife of Pharaoh plucked Moses from the river, saying, "Slay him not, it may be that he will be of use to us." (Quran 28:9)

In the Bible, the daughter of Pharaoh took Moses from the river, sparing his life out of compassion (Exodus 2).

In the Quran, the first miracle assigned to Jesus is the making of a clay bird and then breathing life into it, so it became a living bird. (Quran 3:49).
In the Bible, the first miracle of Jesus performed was turning water into wine at the marriage feast in Cana. (John 2:1-11).

In the Quran, Zechariah is speechless for three nights. (Quran 3:38-41, 19:16-34).
In the Bible, Zechariah is mute from the time the angel speaks to him until after John the Baptist is born (Luke 1).

In the Quran, Jesus was not crucified; instead, it was only made to seem to the witnesses that he was crucified (Quran 4:157).
In the Bible, Jesus was crucified, buried and raised from the dead (Matthew 17, Mark 15, Luke 23, and John 19).

In the Quran, Allah is the holiest name of God. Allah has 99 names in the Quran which shows his attributes and character.
In the Bible, Jehovah is the holiest name of God which is not mentioned in the Quran even one time.

1.5 *Different Ideologies: Muslims believe in Replacement Theology*

According to the teachings of Islam, all the teachings of the old prophets have been cancelled and Muslims do not need to read them because the final revelation has been revealed through

Muhammad and the Quran is the final word of Allah. They believe:

- The Bible has been replaced with the Quran.
- Jesus has been replaced with Muhammad as the greatest prophet.
- Jerusalem has been replaced with Mecca.
- The holy Temple of Solomon has been replaced with Kaba.
- The Law of the Torah has been replaced with the Law of the Quran.
- The Israeli nation has been replaced with Muslims as His 'chosen' people.
- Judaism has been replaced with Islam.
- The Temple has been replaced with the Mosque.
- Muslims say, believe and claim that all Jewish prophets were Muslims from the beginning i.e. Jesus, Abraham and Adam.
- Muslims love the dead Jews and want to live like them but hate the living Jews.

1.6 Summary: Has the God of Abraham changed?

Is God changeable?
"He is the same yesterday, today and forever." (Hebrews 13:8)
God is not a man that he changes his decisions. If a man keeps on changing his decision or will, what kind of person will you think he is? Maybe you will say that he is a cheater, betrayer, not trustworthy or merely one who gives false hope.

1) God said to Abraham, *"Whoever will bless you I will bless them and whoever will curse you I will curse them."* (Genesis 12:3) but Allah said kill all the Jews from the surface of the earth.

39

SAHIH AL BUKHARI, Volume 4, Book 56, Number 791:
Narrated by Abdullah bin Umar: *"I heard Allah's apostle (Muhammad) saying, the Jews will fight with you and you will be given victory over them so that a stone will say, O Muslim! There is a Jew behind me; kill him."*

SAHIH AL BUKHARI, Volume 4, book 52, number 176:
Narrated by Abdullah Bin Umar: Allah's apostle said, *"You (Muslim) will fight with the Jews still some of them will hide behind the tree. The tree will (betray them) saying, O Abdullah! There is a Jew hiding behind me; so kill him."*

2) The God of Abraham said that Jesus is his beloved son with whom he is well pleased. (Matthew 1:11, Matthew 3:17) but Allah says he has no son. (Quran 72:3).

3) The God of Abraham said that killers will not enter into heaven which is His kingdom. (Revelation 22:15) but Allah says whoever will kill the non-Muslims and especially Jews Allah will give him 72 virgins in heaven. (There are 8 references about pertaining to this).

4) The God of Abraham saved the son of Abraham and provided the substitute for his child. (Genesis 22:12-13) but Allah is pleased when people give their children to die in Jihad (Holy War).

5) The God of Abraham said he will not reject Israel. (Romans 11:1, Jeremiah 31: 35-37) but Allah has rejected Israel. (There are many verses in the Hadith).

6) The God of Abraham is unchangeable. He cannot change his mind. (There are 36 verses in the Bible relating to this) but Allah has changed his mind. Mohammedan Law is 85% opposite of the Mosaic Law.

7) God the Father loves the son of Abraham called Isaac and kept his promises with his descendants called Israelites. (Genesis 17:16-17) but Allah loves the son of Abraham called Ishmael and keeps his promises with his descendants called Muslims.

8) Yahweh is the God of all nations and he loves them equally but Allah is only for the Muslims and he has rejected all other nations.

9) The God of Abraham is Yahweh but the God of Islam is Allah which is never ever mentioned in the Torah, by the Major or Minor Prophets, in the books of history, poetry, even in the Gospels or in any other Epistles.

10) The God of Abraham showed himself to Moses and said He is Yahweh, and Yahweh is His most holy name but when the God of Abraham showed himself to Muhammad, he said his name is Allah, which is the holiest name among Muslims (he has changed his identity?).

CHAPTER 2

What is the Truth about Jesus?

(The name and location of this true story has been changed.)

Someone shared the gospel with a man named Lazarus, he believed it and gave his life to Jesus. He became a Christian and he was a secret believer. His family soon discovered that he converted to Christianity; so they conspired to kill him. Lazarus' brother-in-law worked in a zoo and he took home poison from there which they used to eradicate/kill ferocious lions with. One night they forcibly injected Lazarus with the poison, they locked him up a room, believing him to be dead they then informed all their relatives and friends that Lazarus had died and his funeral was to be held "tomorrow at 4pm."

The next day, when they opened the door, to their disbelief they saw Lazarus sitting on his bed praying. He had secured a wound on his right toe and all the poison seeped out through it. His entire family became petrified of him and made the ultimate decision to throw him out of the family home and that he was "never ever" to come back to this village. He left his village and went to Karachi. Whilst in Karachi, he went to numerous pastors requesting water baptism but nobody was willing to baptise him because in Pakistan, it is not safe to baptise a Muslim man unless you are hundred percent sure that he is true seeker. He was very disappointed after two years of struggle trying to get baptised as no one would baptise him. One night he prayed in his room and wept bitterly before the Lord Jesus Christ; he poured out his heart stating that his desire was for a deeper walk with Him but His followers had rejected him and did not want to accept him. He told the Lord his desire to convert back to Islam. Jesus then appeared Lazarus and said to him that if His followers refuse to baptize him then *He* will baptise Lazarus. Jesus instructed him to go to the beach. Lazarus went to the beach as instructed, and at 4am, (as promised), Jesus appeared to him, in physical form, and baptised him. Immediately after the baptism, Jesus disappeared. Today Lazarus goes from village to village and city to city boldly and confidently preaching the gospel of our Lord Jesus Christ.

2.1 *What does the Quran say about Jesus?*

The name of Jesus, his attributes or his teachings are mentioned in the Quran in almost 93 verses. This is not a small number. Christians say that Jesus is the Son of God and Muslims say he is only a prophet and not the son of God. It would seem the Quran proves that He is God. Nobody has seen God; we know Him by his attributes. Here are some of the attributes of Jesus from the Quran which exalts him above a prophet. The Quran has mentioned some of the godly attributes of Jesus which clearly distinguishes Him from a prophet, proving Him to be God.

Creator:
God is the creator of this universe. He created everything just by the power of His words. He commanded and it came to pass.

He breathes and life came into it. The Quran makes it clear in a number of Surahs (chapters) that only Allah has the power to create.

"And those who invoke other than Allah create nothing, and they are created." (Quran 16:20)

"Then is He who creates like one who does not create? So will you not be reminded?" (Quran 16:17)

"That is Allah, your Lord; there is no deity except Him, the creator of all things, so worship him. And he is disposer of all things." (Quran 6:102)

"Indeed, your Lord - He is the knowing creator." (Quran 15:86)

"O people, an example is presented, so listen to it, indeed, those you invoke. Besides Allah will never create (as much as) a fly, even if they gathered together for that purpose." (Surah 22:73)

Time and time again in the Quran, Allah claims that he is the true god and that only he has the power to create. In the Quran, Allah has revealed himself by having 99 names and one of them is "Al-Khaliq" which means the creator. Yet the Quran tells us that the Messiah Jesus Christ also has the power to create.

Quran 3:47-49 says:
"My Lord, how will I have a child when no man has touched me?" (The angel) said, "Such is Allah; He creates what he wills. When he decrees a matter, he only says to it, "Be" and it is. And he will teach him writing and wisdom and the Torah and the Gospel and (make him) a messenger to the children of Israel, (who will say), "indeed I have come to you with a sign from your Lord in that I design for you from clay (that which is) like the form of a bird, then I breathe into it and it becomes a bird by

permission of Allah. And I cure the blind and the leper, and I give life to the dead by permission of Allah. And I inform you of what you eat and what you store in your houses. Indeed in that is a sign for you, if you are believers."

In these verses we see that Jesus has the power to create and he created birds out of clay and breathed life into it as God created Adam in the same way. The Quran says that only God can create. So we see here that Jesus is the creator, God. Jesus breathed life into the birds as God breathed life into Adam.

"Then the Lord God formed a man from the dust of the ground and breathed into his nostrils the breath of life, and the man became a living being." (Genesis 2:7)

Worship:
The Quran commands that only Allah should be worshipped. It also clearly teaches that only Allah is worthy of our worship and we should only bow to him.

One of Allah's names is 'Al-Hamid' which means the praised one. There are stories documented by very reliable Islamic scholars which told that John the Baptist known by the name YAHYA, while in his mother's womb, was said to have bowed down and worshipped Jesus (Isa) while he was in Mary's womb. Al-Qurtubi tells the story like this:

The sister (Elizabeth) visited Mary and said,

"O Mary, do you perceive that I am with child?" Mary answered, "Do you see that I am also with child?" Her sister (Elizabeth) went on, "I feel the child in my womb bowing to the child in your womb."

John (Yahya) was a prophet and a prophet cannot bow down before anyone except God.

Omniscience:
The Quran consistently informs the reader that only Allah is all-

knowing or omniscience.

Quran 3:49 says,
"And I inform you of what you eat and what you store in your house."
Jesus knows the past, present and future. He also says that he knows what you have eaten and what you store in your houses, which proves that he is all-knowing.

Power over Life and Death:
The Quran teaches that only Allah has the power to give life and death. (Quran 15:23, 36:12, 50:43) However, the Quran tells us that Jesus raised the dead and breathed life into the birds from clay.

"I have come to you with a clear sign from your Lord: in your very presence, I make the likeness of a bird out of clay and breathe into it and it becomes, by God's command, a bird. I heal those born blind and the lepers and I bring to life the dead by God's command." (Quran 3:49)

Healer:
The Quran consistently tells us that only Allah is the healer. (Quran 26:80, 6:17)

Even Hadith also states that:
"Whenever Allah's messenger, Muhammad, paid a visit to a patient or a patient was brought to Him, he used to invoke Allah, saying, take away the disease, O the Lord of the people! Cure him as you are the one who cures. There is no cure but yours, a cure that leaves no disease."
We learn from the Quran that Jesus had the power to heal.
"... and I cure the blind and the leper and I give life to the dead by God's command..." (Quran 3:49)

The Judge:
The Quran teaches that Allah is our judge. (Quran 6:57, 7:87,

6:114) The Hadith says that Jesus will judge mankind.

SAHIH AL BUKHARI, vol. 4, book 55, no. 657:
"By him in whose hands my soul is, surely (Jesus) the son of Mary will soon descend amongst you and will judge mankind justly."

God Speaks in Parables:
The Quran asserts strongly that only Allah talks in Parables. (Quran 24:35, 14:25). Jesus Christ spoke quite often in parables or examples to deliver profound spiritual truths. By some estimates Jesus gave 33 to 60 unique parables in the Bible.

Holy:
The Quran talks about the dialogue between the angel and Mary when he came to give good news regarding the birth of Jesus to her. Quran 19:19-21 says,

"He said, I am only the messenger of your Lord to give you (news of) a holy boy. She said, How can I have a boy while no man has touched me and I have not been unchaste? He said, thus (it will be); your Lord says, it is easy for me and we will make him a sign to the people and a mercy from us. And it is a matter (already) decreed. These verses reveal another attribute of Jesus that He is pure and holy. Even Muhammad also mentioned about the holiness and purity of Jesus Christ."

Hadith volume 4, book 55, page 641 and vol. 6, book 60, page 71: Abu Huraira reported: *"The messenger of Allah, peace and blessings is upon him, said, No person is born but that he is pricked by Satan and he cries from the touch of Satan, except for Mary and her son (Isa)."*

In the light of this Hadith, we know that the life of Jesus Christ was the holiest in all of the human beings and among all the prophets who came in this world. This Hadith reveals that Jesus was the greatest prophet among all the prophets who ever lived and was the holiest person on this earth. He was an unblemished person throughout the whole of human history; an incomparable person who is unique in his character and sayings, superior above all of those who came before Him and most certainly after Him - Satan could not parallel himself against Him. That is the standard of His holiness and Satan cannot come near to Him because He is holy God.

Mercy:
He (the angel) said, "Thus (it will be); your Lord says, it is easy for me and we will make him (Isa) a sign to the people and a mercy from us. And it is a matter (already) decreed. One of Allah's names is Al-Rahman which means Mercy/Merciful." (Quran 19:21)

The Word of Truth:
"That is Jesus, the son of Mary - The Word of Truth about which they are in dispute." (Quran 19:34)

The Word of God:
Jesus is referred to as the 'Word of God' in two passages in the Quran. No prophet has been described with such a title.

When the angel said, "O Mary, indeed Allah gives you good tidings of a Word from Him, whose name will be the Messiah, Jesus, the son of Mary - distinguished in this world and the hereafter and among those brought near (to Allah)." (Quran 3:45)

"O people of the Scripture, do not commit excess in your religion or say about Allah except the truth. The Messiah, Jesus, the Son of Mary, was but a messenger of Allah and His Word which He directed to Mary and a spirit from Him." (Quran 4:171)

These verses reveal Jesus as the 'Word of God.' The Bible says in John 1:1-3 *"In the beginning was the Word, and the Word was with God, and the Word was God. He was with God in the beginning. Through him all things were made; without him nothing was made that has been made."*

The Spirit of God:
The Quran describes Jesus as the spirit of God.

"And the one who guarded her chastity, so we blew (spirit) into her through our angel (Gabriel), and we made her and her son a sign for the world." (Quran 21:91)

"And Mary, the daughter of Imran, who guarded her chastity, so we blew (spirit) into her through our angel, and she believed in the words of her Lord and His scriptures and was of the devoutly obedient." (Quran 66:22)

"O people of the Scripture, so not commit excess in your religion or say about Allah except the truth. The Messiah, Jesus, the son of Mary, was but a messenger of Allah and His word which He directed to Mary and a spirit from Him." (Quran 4:171)

2.2 *What does the Bible say about Jesus?*

John 14:9 says, *"He who has seen me has seen the Father."* Nobody has seen God. We know Him through His attributes.

Creator:
John 1:3 says, *"Through Him all things were made; without him nothing was made that has been made."* He is a God of creation. He created the world and all that is in it.

Worship:
Revelation 19:10 says, *"At this I fell at his feet to worship him. But he said to me, don't do that! I am a fellow servant with you and with your brothers and sisters who hold to the testimony of Jesus. Worship God!"* An angel instructed the apostle John to only worship God.

Several times in scripture Jesus has received worship from other people:

- Matthew 2:11 – *"The three wise men bowed down and worshipped Jesus."*
- Matthew 14:33 – *"When Jesus came into the boat, the wind died down. Then those who were in the boat worshipped him."* (The apostles)
- Matthew 28:9 – *"Suddenly Jesus met them. Greetings! He said. They came to him, clasped his feet and worshipped him."* (Apostles after resurrection)
- Luke 24:52 – *"Then they worshipped him and returned to Jerusalem with great joy."* (Before ascension)
- John 9:38 – *"He said, Lord, I believe, and he worshipped him."* (A blind man who was healed by Jesus.)

Jesus never ever rebuked people for worshiping Him. He did not correct them or say, "Don't you realise that I am just a mortal prophet? Stop worshiping me!" As the angel in Revelation commanded that no worship be given to him.

Omnipresent:
John 1:48 says, *"How do you know me?" Nathaniel asked. Jesus answered, "I saw you while you were still under the fig tree before Philip called you."*

Omniscience:
- Jesus knew that Lazarus has died. (John 11:14)

51

- Jesus knew that He would die and will rise again from the dead.
- Jesus knew about the Samaritan women that she was not living with her husband.
- Jesus knew that Peter would deny Him three times that he knows Him.

Omnipotent:
- Jesus raised the dead.
- Jesus forgave sins.
- Jesus healed the blind, lame and deaf.
- Jesus seized the storm.

2.3 *Did Jesus claim to be God?*

Most Muslims say that Jesus never said in the gospels that he is God. Jesus came to reveal the Father – that is why he said, *"He who has seen me has seen the Father."* Now we will see some of the claims that Jesus made.

John 5:18 says, *"For this cause therefore the Jews were seeking all the more to kill Him, because he not only was breaking the Sabbath, but also was calling God his own father, making himself equal with God."*

The Jewish religious leaders of his time understood that Jesus claimed to be God that is why they wanted to kill him. Here are two claims which infuriated the Jewish leaders and unsettled them greatly:

- He was calling God His own Father.
- He was making himself parallel or equal with God.

John 10:30-33 says, *"Again the Jews picked up stones to stone Him,"* but Jesus said to them, *"I have shown you many great miracles from the Father, for which of these do you stone me? We are not stoning you for any of these,"* replied the Jews, *"but for blasphemy because you are a mere man claiming to be God."*

Jesus claimed to be God that's why the Jewish people tried to stone him for this very reason:

John 8:58 says, *"Jesus declared, "I tell you the truth... before Abraham was born, I am."*

This is a powerful claim from Jesus. First, that he pre-existed his human birth. Second, that he was actually alive and present before Abraham. When the Jews heard such inflammatory statements they acknowledged it to be blasphemy.

John 1:1 says, *"In the beginning was the Word, the word was with God and the Word was God."*

Here, the word 'beginning' means 'eternity past.' Before anything was created Jesus was there. These verses clearly indicate that Jesus is eternal.

John 20:28 says, *"Thomas said to him, "My Lord and My God."*
When Thomas the disciple declared concerning Jesus, *"My Lord and My God"*, he declared his true identity. Jesus did not correct him or rebuke him but accepted this declaration.

No human being can make these kinds of claims that:

• God is His own Father.
• He is equal with God.
• He is God.

- He is Eternal God.
- He is Lord and God.

2.4 *How can Jesus be the Son of God?*

Firstly, we need to recognise and understand that Christians do not believe the same way Muslims believe i.e. that Jesus is the Son of God.

Christians believe that God is one as it is written in 1 Timothy 2:5, *"For there is one God and one mediator between God and mankind, the man Christ Jesus."* Galatians 3:20 states, 'A mediator' exists. However, this implies more than one party; but God is one. Many Muslims believe that the Christian faith is that Jesus is the physical son of God. That is why Muslims deny and say that God has no son because he has no wife.

"(He is) originator of the heavens and the earth. How could he have a son when he doesn't have a wife and he created all things? And he is, if all things, knowing." (Quran 6:101)

Muslims think that Christians believe that God had sexual intercourse with Mary hence the reason why Jesus is called the Son of God. Nauzubillah! Means 'I seek refuge from Allah from that thing.' This is sin. As Christians we do not believe that God had sexual relations with Mary, that is why Jesus is called the Son of God. Jesus is not a physical son of God but an eternal and spiritual Son of God. As it is written in Romans 1:3-4, *"Regarding his son, who as to his earthly life was a descendant of David, and who through the spirit of holiness was appointed the son of God in power by his resurrection from the dead: Jesus Christ our Lord."*

Muslims have no idea why or how Christians believe that Jesus is the Son of God. For having a son God does not need a wife. The 'Son' title is used in an intimate relationship. There are two ingredients needed here: fellowship and relationship. Our fellowship can break but our relationship cannot break. Consider the following example, imagine if I have an altercation with my father, and then decide in a huff to move abroad, severing all contact with him to the point that he has no idea of my whereabouts or any difficulties that I am daily encountering. And if someone should ask me about him, do you think that I would respond that he is not my father because I no longer have a relationship with him? No.

Wherever I will go in the world, he is still my father. I may not be in physical contact, be thousands of miles away from him and on both sides we do not know anything about each other's lives and or communication has totally ceased. However, our fellowship can break but our relationship is unbreakable. He is my father and he will be my father forever. Muslims use many terms for son and here I want to use some Muslim terminology and consider some questions.

Muslims frequently use the word 'Ibn-e-Sabeel' which means 'son of the road.' Someone who is a traveller and continually moves from one place to another is referred as the Son of the Road. It does not mean that his father or mother had some sexual relations with the road so that's not why he was called the Son of the Road. Another name often used is 'Abu Jahal' which means 'father of ignorance.' Now here, you can ask a question, does ignorance have a wife? Clearly they will say no. This is just one of his attributes because he did many foolish things.

Another term which many Muslims use is 'Son of Lion'. If someone is very sturdy and courageous then they call him Son of Lion. They refer to him in this way because of his attributes and not because his father was a lion or his mother had sexual relations with a lion.

The Prophet Muhammad gave new names to some of his disciples like: Hazrat Abu Bakr Sadeq. Abu Bakr means father of goats. Then you can ask the obvious question, did he have some sort of sexual relations with the goats? Hence, why he was called the father of goats? They will answer a clear no. This title was given because of his love for goats so that is why he got the title, 'Father of Goats'.

Another name that Muhammad gave to one of his disciples was: 'Abu Huraira' which means 'Father of Cats'. The same sequence of questions can be applied, "Did he have sexual relations with cats to address him as the Father of Cats?" Again, they will say no and will answer, it was because he loved his cats so much that is why he received the title, Father of Cats.

So then you can explain to them that when we say that Jesus is the Son of God, there is no sexual relations involved whatsoever. Emphasise that the term 'son' is not only derived out of sexual relations, which is more important.

So when we say that Jesus is the Son of God, there are no sexual relations involved. Jesus is called the Son of God because of His holiness - Romans 1:3-4 says, *"Regarding His Son, who as to His earthly life was a descendant of David, and who through the spirit of holiness was appointed the Son of God in power by His resurrection from the dead: Jesus Christ our Lord."*

Jesus was called the Son of God because of his holiness.

2.5 *Did Jesus say He was the Son of God?*

Over the years, Muslims have said to me that if I can show them one reference from the Bible, where Jesus states that He is the Son of God then immediately, without hesitation, they will convert to Christianity. Most of the Muslims who ask this question do not know anything about the Bible and they ask this question out of their ignorance.

Let me give you some references from the New Testament where Jesus is mentioned as the son of God.

God said that Jesus is the Son of God:

"And a voice from heaven said, "This is my son, whom I love; with him I am well pleased." (Matthew 3:17)

While he was still speaking, a bright cloud covered them, and a voice from the cloud said, "This is my son, whom I love; with him I am well pleased. Listen to him!" (Matthew 17:5)

"And the Holy Spirit descended on him in bodily form like a dove. And a voice came from heaven: "You are my son, whom I love; with you I am well pleased." (Luke 3:22)

"While he was speaking, a cloud appeared and covered them, they were afraid as they entered the cloud. A voice came from the cloud, saying, "This is my son, whom I have chosen; listen to him." (Luke 9:35)

Jesus Acknowledged that He is the Son of God:

Jesus replied, "If I glorify myself, my glory means nothing, My Father, whom you claim as your God, is the one who glorifies me." (John 8:54)

But Jesus remained silent and has no answer. Again the High Priest asked him, "Are you the Messiah, the son of the blessed one?" "I am," Jesus said. And you will see the Son of man sitting at the right hand of the Mighty One and coming on the clouds of heaven." (Mark 14:61-62)

"Then they asked, are you then the son of God?" He replied, "You say that I am." (Luke 22:70)

"In His defence Jesus said to them, "My Father is always at his work to this very day, and I too am working." For this reason they tried all the more to kill him; Not only was he breaking the Sabbath, but he was even calling God his own Father, making himself equal with God." (John 5: 17-18)

"When he heard this, Jesus said, "This sickness will not end in death. No, it is for God's glory so that God's son may be glorified through it." (John 11:4)

"Jesus said, "Do not hold on to me, for I have not yet ascended to the Father. Go instead to my brothers and tell them, "I am ascending to my Father and your Father, to my God and your God." (John 20:17)

The Angel Gabriel said that Jesus is the Son of God:
"He will be great and will be called the Son of the Most High God. The Lord God will give him the throne of his father David." (Luke 1:32)

The angel answered, "The Holy Spirit will come on you, and the power of the Most High God will overshadow you. So the Holy one to be born will be called the Son of God." (Luke 1:35)

John the Baptist said that Jesus is the Son of God:
"I have seen and I testify that this is the son of God." (John 1:34)

The Disciples said that Jesus is the Son of God:
"Then those who were in the boat worshiped him, saying, "Truly you are the son of God." (Matthew 14:33)

Simon Peter said that Jesus is the Son of God:
Simon Peter answered, *"You are the Messiah, the son of the living God."* (Matthew 16:16)

John said that Jesus is the Son of God:
"But these are written that you may believe that Jesus is the Messiah, the son of God, and that by believing you may have life in his name."
(John 20:31)

Martha said that Jesus is the Son of God:
"Yes, Lord," she replied, "I believe that you are the Messiah, the Son Of God, who is to come into the world." (John 11:27)

Nathaniel said that Jesus is the Son of God:
"Then Nathaniel declared, "Rabbi, you are the son of God; you are the king of Israel." (John 1:49)

The Centurion said that Jesus is the Son of God:
"When the centurion and those with him who were guarding Jesus saw the earthquake and all that had happened, they were terrified, and exclaimed, "Surely he was the Son of God!" (Matthew 27:54)

Demons said that Jesus is the Son of God:
"What do you want with us, the son of God?" they shouted. "Have you come here to torture us before the appointed time?"
(Matthew 8:29)

"Moreover, demons came out of many people, shouting, "You are the son of God!" But he rebuked them and would not allow them to speak, because they knew he was the Messiah." (Luke 4:41)

"When he saw Jesus, he cried out and fell at his feet, shouting at the top of his voice, "What do you want with me, Jesus, Son of the Most High God? I beg you, don't torture me!" (Luke 8:28)

Satan said that Jesus is the Son of God:
"The tempted came to him and said, "If you are the son of God, tell these stones to become bread." (Matthew 4:3)

"The devil led him to Jerusalem and had him stand on the highest point of the Temple. "If you are the son of God," he said, "Throw yourself down from here." (Luke 4:9)

The Angel Gabriel, John the Baptist, Disciples of Jesus, Simon Peter, John, Martha, Nathaniel, The Centurion, Demons and even Satan identified Jesus as the Son of God.

2.6 *Is Jesus just a prophet?*

Muslims adamantly believe and the Quran teaches that Jesus was 'just' a prophet of Allah. Was Jesus an ordinary man? Was Jesus just a prophet? Was Jesus a great religious leader only? Was he more than a spiritual hero? These are questions which have been asked for more than two thousand years since he was born in Bethlehem. These questions are still being asked by billions of people around the world.

If Jesus was just an ordinary man, or a prophet, or a leader, or a spiritual hero then He would not have been able to change the entire world. He would not have been able to lay the foundation of the church. He would not have been able to train twelve people who turned this world upside down.

Let me share something about the life of Jesus with you. Jesus was a perfect man and perfect God.

I will explain later that if Jesus is God then why was he praying, and to whom was he praying? Why he died. Why he was crying. Why he used to sleep or why he had to be born (from a woman.) He was called the Son of God and a son of man. How he had authority to forgive sins. He had authority to raise the dead and authority over nature. He is the Saviour of this world.

He is Christ, the promised Messiah.

Titles of Christ:
Jesus Christ was born in Bethlehem, Israel. There are so many titles in the scriptures which were given to Jesus such as: The Word of God, The Son of Man, The Son of God, the Healer of this World, a great teacher and so many more.
 He was a perfect symbol of self-control, but he was not isolated from this world. He lived in this world but did not pursue its laws and values. He had human and divine nature. He lived a holy life and even his adversaries could find no fault in Him (John 8:4-6). Even the judge said, "*I don't find any wrong in Him*" (John 19:6). He was the greatest, humblest and meekest person to ever walk the face of this world. He washed his disciples' feet and made himself as a servant. He was a great expression of God's love on this earth. He is and was the ultimate symbol of love and mercy in action.

Claims of Christ:
The Lord Jesus Christ not only proved Himself to be holy, a sin free person, but claimed that He had the authority to forgive sins, which only God can forgive. According to the scriptures, only God has power to forgive but Jesus demonstrated this too.
 Jesus claimed that He has power to give life: "*For just as the father raises the dead and gives them life, even so the Son gives life to whom he is pleased to give it.*" (John 5:21).
 Jesus claimed that He is The Bread of Life: "*Then Jesus declared, I am the bread of life. Whoever comes to me will never go hungry, and whoever believes in me will never be thirsty.*" (John 6:35).
 Jesus claimed that He is The Resurrection and Eternal Life: "*Jesus said to her, "I am the resurrection and the life. The one who believes in me will live, even though they die.*" (John 11:25).
 Jesus claimed that He pre-existed, even before He was born and said that He was even before Abraham: "*Very truly I tell you, Jesus*

answered, before Abraham was born, I am!" (John 5:58).

Jesus claimed that He is the Light of the World: *"While I am in the world, I am the light of the world."* (John 9:5).

Jesus claimed that He is the gate and nobody goes to heaven except through Him: *"Therefore Jesus said again, "Very truly I tell you, I am the gate for the sheep. I am the gate; whoever enters through me will be saved, they will come in and go out and find pasture."* (John 10:7, 9).

Jesus claimed that he came to give life and life of abundance: *"The thief comes only to steal and kill and destroy; I have come that they may have life, and have it to the full."* (John 10:10).

Jesus claimed that no one goes to God except through Him: *"Jesus answered, I am the Way and the truth and the life. No one comes to the Father except through me."* (John 14:6)

Jesus claimed that He will judge the world. *"Moreover, the Father judges no one, but he entrusted all judgment to the Son, that all may honour the Son, just as they honour the father, who sent him. Very truly I tell you; whoever hears my word and believes him who sent me has entered life and will not be judged but has crossed over from death to life."* (John 5:22-24).

Jesus accepted the title of Lord and God:
"Now Thomas (also known as Didymium), one of the twelve, was not with the disciples when Jesus came. So the other disciples told him, "we have seen the Lord!" But said to them, "unless I see the nail marks in His hands and put my finger where the nails were, and put my hand into His side, I will not believe." A week later his disciples were in the house again, and Thomas was with them. Though the doors were locked, Jesus came and stood among them and said, "Peace is with you!" then he said to Thomas, "put your finger here; see my hands. Reach out your hand and put it into my side. Stop doubting and believe." Thomas said to him, "My Lord and my God!" (John 20:26-28). Jesus didn't correct him or rebuke him but accepted this declaration. When John the disciple of Jesus fell at the feet of an angel and worshiped him, the

angel stopped him. But Jesus did not stop Thomas.

"At this I fell at his (an angel's) feet to worship him. But he said to me, "Don't do that! I am a fellow servant with you and with your brothers and sisters who hold to the testimony of Jesus. Worship God!" (Revelation 19:10)

Here the angel instructed the apostle John to only worship God. Several times in the scriptures Jesus has received worship from other people:

"The three wise man bowed down and worshiped Jesus." (Matthew 2:11)

"When Jesus came into the boat, the wind died down. Then those who (the apostles) were in the boat worshiped him." (Matthew 14:33)

"Suddenly Jesus met them. Greetings! He said. They came to Him, clasped his feet and worshiped Him." (Matthew 28:9)

"He said, Lord, I believe, and he worshiped him." A blind man who was healed by Jesus. (John 9:38)

Jesus never rebuked people for worshipping Him. Neither did He correct them or openly declare: "Don't you realise that I am just a mortal prophet? Stop worshipping me!" No, he never embraced that because he recognised that people knew who He was. This is in direct contrast to the angel in the book of Revelation who vehemently commanded the Apostle John not to worship him.

The Life Story of our Lord Jesus Christ:
Now I will present a concise life story of our Lord Jesus Christ which is unlike what the Quran teaches. The Lord Jesus Christ was born in Bethlehem by a virgin, Mary. He was born like any other child

under the law but was born in a manger. When he was born, the angelic host appeared and sang joyful songs and praised God. The shepherds came and worshiped Him. Three kings came and kneeled down before Him and presented him with numerous gifts.

He lived a perfect sinless life. For thirty years of His life he lived in Nazareth and worked there as a carpenter. At the age of thirty, He commenced preaching that mankind was to *"repent, for the kingdom of heaven has come near."*

He performed countless miracles such as: raising the dead; miraculously opening the eyes of the blind; opening the ears of the deaf; He healed the dumb; completely cleansed lepers and He cast out demons. With death curdling fury the Jewish leaders arrested Him in a fit of jealousy and indignation; they presented him before the Roman rulers.

One of his own disciples betrayed him and handed Him over to the Jewish leaders. The Jewish leaders falsely accused Him but they were not able to prove any accusation. Then the Jewish leaders handed Him over to the Romans who lashed him 39 times on His back. The Roman soldiers put a crown of thorns on His head, they spat in His face and callously wrenched out His beard. They mocked Him. They mounted a heavy cross on His shoulders for Him to carry. He hauled His cross to Mount of Calvary, the final destination, where they crucified Him.

Whilst nailed to the cross, He requested water to quench His dying thirst but they denied His request, giving him vinegar to drink instead. The Roman soldiers pierced his side and witnessed an overflow of water and blood spewing out. Hanging on the cross, He forgave all those who had persecuted Him. In utter discomfort and unspeakable pain He prayed, crying loudly for His tormentors: *"Father, forgive them, they know nothing."* He died on the cross and later they buried Him according to the Jewish customs. After three days, Jesus rose from the dead as He had told His disciples that He would. After His resurrection, He kept appearing to His disciples for a further forty days. After forty days, He ascended to heaven where He is seated at the right hand of the Father. He will come back again to judge the whole world. He will reward the righteous with eternal life and will punish the sinners in hell for eternity.

2.7 Are there three Gods?

This objection is made because of the lack of knowledge about the Christian faith and teachings of Christ. The Bible teaches us that God is one.

"Hear, O Israel: The LORD our God, The LORD is one." (Deuteronomy 6:4)

Jesus acknowledged and said the same thing in Mark 12:29, *"Jesus answered, "The most important is, Hear, O Israel: The LORD our God, The LORD is one."* Jesus taught that God is one.

"And the scribe said to him, "You are right, Teacher. You have truly said that he is one, and there is no other besides him." (Mark 12:32)

So the Bible teaches that God is one but He has revealed Himself in three persons: God the Father, God the Son and God the Holy Spirit - but still they are one being. So it doesn't mean that there are three Gods. The Bible teaches us that God is three in one. For a non-Christian believer, it is very difficult to understand the expression of Father, Son and Holy Spirit. Actually, God revealed Himself into these expressions for our understanding because with our human mind, it is very easy to understand these expressions. This is God's amazing grace that he has shown mercy to the limited human mind and knowledge.

For Christians, it is not an easy job to explain the trinity to non-Christians. In the first stage, if you accept it by faith then God will give you his supernatural revelation and divine wisdom to understand it but if you try to understand it by your carnal mind, you will never comprehend it; it is impossible.

For those attempting to decode the trinity with their carnal minds make very common mistakes. They try to understand it with mathematical formulas. Nevertheless, if we use the right formulas then we can get the right answer otherwise we will not be able to solve the problem.

Mostly non-believers try to decipher it with the addition method. For example 1+1+1=3. This is the wrong method. The Biblical calculation method is not addition but of multiplication. God said to Adam and Eve, multiply and be fruitful. God did not say add in number and be fruitful, but if you use the multiplication method then the answer will be right. For example 1×1×1=1. The trinity is not to present the quantity of Gods, but to reveal God to the level and understanding of the human mind.

Let me put it this way, everything in this world has been based on the trinity. God created man in his own image and man is based on the trinity: body, spirit and soul. It does not mean that there are three separate men. Another example to consider is an egg. An egg is based on the trinity i.e. the shell, white and yoke. Again, it does not mean that there are three eggs. Let us ponder the universe; it is based on the following: heaven, earth and space. It does not mean that there are three universes. An atom is miniscule yet it has its DNA fashioned on the trinity: electron, proton and neutron. It does not mean that there are three atoms. So Christians do not worship three gods but one God, the true and eternal God, who is the God of Abraham, Isaac and Jacob.

CHAPTER 3

What happened to Jesus?

I recall an emotive event that happened when my family and I lived in Pakistan. One day, I dropped my wife and daughter to my mother's house as I went onto a cell group meeting. Shortly after I arrived, my wife telephoned me to report that our daughter was "missing." I was not overly concerned but added, "She will be in somebody's house, go and check." Satisfied, I went back to the meeting. However, time lapsed and four hours later my daughter was still absent. My wife updated me that she had checked everywhere in the houses of family members of the church; relatives and friends, but our daughter was still missing. Gradually fear and anxiety began to seize me. Where was my daughter?

A frantic search began. I checked hospitals, police stations and virtually any and everywhere I believe that she could be. My search was all in vain. When I returned at midnight I was despondent. I saw my wife waiting eagerly to see me return with our daughter. When she saw me empty handed she started crying and I also started crying. I consoled her telling her that our daughter is "in somebody's hands." I concluded, "Only God can bring our daughter back safe and sound." There were family members and friends in our house also waiting and I implored for us to all start praying. We started praying at midnight till 5am non-stop.

When we were praying some of the friends suggested that we go and search for her. But I said to my wife that only God can help us and can bring back our daughter. We did not listen to the friend's suggestion but kept praying, while we continued my wife received a call. It was the lady who had kidnapped our daughter. She told my wife that our daughter was with her. My wife on hearing the news shouted to the group that she had been found! I took the phone from my wife and calmly spoke to the lady. She confirmed to me that she has my daughter but that they were very fearful. Interestingly, this was something that we were praying, that God would put fear into their hearts. I said to the lady that we are Christians and we honour our words. So we will not do anything against them but we simply want our daughter back safe and sound.

The female kidnapper gave me an address and told me to arrive unaccompanied. My brother was present and vehemently objected to her request; he and numerous others would accompany me. So we went - 20 to 25 people in four cars. However, I was driving alone and they were following behind, at some distance, in order not to arouse suspicion. When we reached the first address nobody was there. It was vacant. She proceeded to give us four different addresses; these were false flags as she was not at any of them. Finally, she provided a fifth address. When we arrived I saw the lady, she stood there with my daughter standing alone in the road. When I parked my car in front of the lady, immediately three unknown cars proceeded to block my car - from the front, the back and the right hand side - the left hand side was a footpath. So my car was wedged in.

When the other cars arrived, that were following me, they in turn also pulled up. I stepped out of my car grabbed my daughter and quickly ran back to my car. During this time one of my cousins went to that lady and started arguing with her, his emotions erupted. She told him they took my daughter because of my evangelistic activities and because they wanted to "teach me a lesson."

When we arrived back home, my daughter was traumatized; she could not speak for some time, she communicated her feelings by simply crying. She was not able to talk to us, she remained in her room, she lost her appetite and refused to play with her younger sister. Looking at her in pain and hurting broke my heart and I wept bitterly, I would cry and cry; the anger and undiluted rage that rose up only fuelled my hatred for the kidnappers. I wanted revenge. I wanted to kill those people but each time I was angry God would say, "Forgive those people." Each time I replied, "God, Father! I can't forgive."

One day God said to me, "You can forgive but you don't want to forgive." Contemplating, I then replied, 'God, okay Father please help me to forgive those people." As soon as I uttered those words: "Father I forgive," I noticed that my daughter started getting better. A week later she was healed! She told us exactly what happened to her. She told us that the female kidnapper had a gun and if my daughter made a sound - even "from your throat" - then the female kidnapper swore that she would kill her. My daughter asked for food from the lady. She threatened my daughter not to ask again as such a request will result in her being killed, so she could not ask for anything. One week, after saying the forgiveness prayer, my daughter's life was back to normal. Glory to God now and forever! Amen.

3.1 *Did Jesus really die on the cross?*

This is very a serious question for thousands of people, but for Christians it is a foolish question because they know and believe in the crucifixion of our Lord Jesus Christ based on the religious and historical proof.

For the answer to this question, we need to look into the Bible because the Bible is the foundation of the Christian faith. The gospels emphasise the crucifixion of our Lord Jesus Christ, and clearly tell us that Christ not only died on the cross but was buried and rose from the dead on the third day. The scriptures tell us, *"Christ died for our sins, buried and rose from the dead on the third day according to the scriptures."* (1 Corinthians 15:4)

It is not enough to believe this just because it is written in any book. So that is why we need to look into this question critically and then we will examine whether it is true or false.

It is very important for us to look into the historical books of Romans and Hebrews. Many Roman and Hebrew secular historical books reveal that the founder of Christianity, Jesus Christ, was crucified on mount of Calvary. Many Roman and Hebrew secular writers have written of the biography of Jesus Christ and in their books they have mentioned the death of Christ in a very detailed account.

The cross of our Lord Jesus Christ is a strong pillar in the Christian faith. If we take the cross out of Christianity then it is a just a shallow building which can collapse at any time. This building cannot stand without the cross.

According to Biblical teaching, the cross of Christ is God's way of forgiving our sins and giving us new life and a new relationship with Him. The cross of our Lord Jesus Christ reveals the result of sin, the separation from God, and meaningless and purposeless life. Let me tell you that when Adam and Eve fell into sin, God was not just an observer of this painful and horrible drama. Actually God intervened into this whole situation and played an active role, because of sin, God and Adam's fellowship was broken and they were separated from each other. For the restoration of this fellowship God sent his Son, the Lord Jesus Christ, who died on the cross and paid for the sins of human beings.

God did it out of His love. The cross of our Lord Jesus Christ is a symbol of God's love. On the cross - love and holiness embraced and kissed each other. That is why the love of God came down to earth and lifted up the rejected one on high.

3.2 Christ was not crucified; someone else hung on the cross instead of Christ.

In the second century, there were so many occultists who believed that Jesus was not human but only God. So being God, Jesus cannot die (we will look into this question separately) because nobody can crucify God. According to the occult, Jesus was not crucified so that is why he was not dead, but they believed that someone died on the cross but they had no answer to this question who exactly it was who died on the cross. But soon after, this occult died by itself.

Six hundred years later, this occult (or belief) came to life and Islam gave new life to this occult belief. Islam represented this occult belief: *"Because Jesus was a holy and beloved prophet of Allah so that's why Allah didn't want his prophet to suffer on the cross because it was a great disgrace for the prophet."* So that's why Allah didn't allow this to happen with Jesus. That's why Allah took him to heaven and someone else was crucified on his behalf and who was that person? In Islam they have different views about it.

"And (we cursed them) for their disbelief and their saying against Mary a great slander, and (for) their saying, "indeed, we have killed the Messiah, Jesus, the son of Mary, the messenger of Allah," and they didn't kill him, nor did they crucify him; but (another) was made to resemble him to them. And indeed, those who differ over it are in doubt about it. They have no knowledge of it except the following of assumption. And they

didn't kill him, for certain. Rather, Allah raised him to himself. And ever is Allah exalted in Might and Wise." (Quran 4:156-158)

So here is the question, who was that person who was crucified? In Islam, there are three different views:

The first group of people believe that he was John, the beloved disciple, of Jesus. According to the Islamic traditions, when Jesus was with his disciples at the last supper, all his disciples were there. Jesus asked his disciples, "Who among you want to go to heaven first?" Then John, the beloved disciple, said that he wanted to go to heaven first. Then Jesus gave his image to him and the Roman soldiers arrested John and crucified him.

Very easily, we can prove that this ideology is wrong because when Jesus was crucified, Jesus gave the responsibility of his mother to John and asked John to look after his mother. After that, John preached the gospel and he wrote one gospel account and three epistles as well. In the end, John wrote the book of Revelation which talks about the end time events. So this person who died on the cross was not John the beloved disciple of Jesus but Jesus himself.

The second view is that it was Judas Iscariot, who betrayed Jesus. He was crucified on the cross instead of Christ. This view argues that Judas Iscariot resembled Christ, so that is why the Roman soldiers arrested Judas Iscariot and crucified him on the cross. They believe that Christians are deceived. This is also a false view, because Judas Iscariot was the one who went to the Jewish leaders and confessed his sin before them and said that they arrested an innocent man. Later he committed suicide by hanging himself on a tree. These questions remain: If Judas Iscariot was crucified on the cross then who then hanged him on the tree? If Judas was crucified on the cross then why did he remain silent and not speak out before Pilate and confess that he was not Christ? Why did he not tell the Jewish leaders that he was not Christ but their friend who helped them to arrest Christ? The soldiers beat him but he didn't tell them. When they nailed Jesus' hands and feet why did he remain so quiet? Why did he not shout that he was Judas Iscariot? Some people say that when the Roman soldiers came to arrest Jesus, Allah gave Jesus' image to Judas Iscariot and they arrested him. In this way, they include Allah as well in this deceptive act. If Allah did so then Allah was part of this deception. Did God deceive? No, God cannot deceive anybody.

Job 34:10-12 says,
"So listen to me, you men of understanding, far be it from God to do evil, from the Almighty to do wrong. He repays everyone for what they have done; he brings on them what their conduct deserves. It is unthinkable that God would do wrong, that the Almighty would pervert justice."

So remember, God cannot deceive anybody.

Abdul Majid Dariabadi, a Muslim scholar, wrote the exegesis of the Quran and he argues the person who was crucified on the cross was not Judas Iscariot but Simon Carini, who carried the cross for Jesus. He wrote that in that time, every criminal used to carry his own cross. When Simon carried the cross for Christ, the Roman soldiers mistook him for the criminal so that is why they took him and crucified him on the cross.

Questions remain: Firstly, were the Roman soldiers foolish that they took the cross from off the criminal and ignored him and let him run away? Secondly, at which point did Jesus Christ escape? Or is it the character of a prophet to have a scapegoat? Can any prophet escape and let any innocent person die on his behalf? Can any prophet harm any person and can be silent? Finally, when the Roman soldiers were crucifying Simon Carini, why did he not shout that he is not Christ? Why did he remain mute?

To reject all these theories, we cannot expect that John, the beloved disciple, or Judas Iscariot, or Simon Carini can say to the robber who was crucified on the cross, next to them, that *"Today you will be with me in paradise."* Nor John, Judas or Simon can say from the cross *"Father, forgive them, they know not what they do."* Judas Iscariot could not say that because he himself deceived his master and leader. Even John couldn't say that because he himself was begging to go to heaven. Nor Simon Carini, could say that because he did not know the teaching and authority of Christ.

Only Muslim scholars support this theory. Most of them support their arguments with reference to the Gospel according to Barnabas, which is a fake gospel account. This gospel was written in the fourteenth century. In this gospel it is mentioned that Judas Iscariot was crucified on the cross instead of Jesus Christ. Every Christian believer who has read this gospel has declared that this is a counterfeit gospel account. (If you want to read more about it then please see Barkat A.Khan's book, 'Discussion on the gospel of Barnabas').

It is impossible to believe that the person who was crucified on the cross was not Christ because of the seven statements which Jesus made from the cross. Nobody who is nailed to the cross by mistake can make these statements.

The seven statements of Christ are as follows:
"Father, forgive them, for they know not what they are doing."
(Luke 23:34)

"Truly, I say to you, today, you will be with me in paradise."
(Luke 23:43)

"Woman, behold, your son: son, behold your mother." (John 19:26-27)

"My God, my God, why have you forsaken me?" (Matthew 27:46, Mark 15:34)

"I thirst." (John 19:28)

"It is finished." (John 19:30)

"Father into your hands I commit my spirit." (Luke 23:46)

These seven statements of Christ are occupied with love, compassion, purity and grace which are the character of Christ. So we can safely conclude that the person who was crucified on the cross with nails, pounded into his hands and feet, was none other than Christ. He gave His life on the cross for our sins to rescue us from the slavery of sin and the bondage of Satan, to give us eternal life and to restore the relationship which was broken by the sin of Adam.

3.3 Christ was crucified but did not die on the cross, he was just unconscious.

Only Ahmeddia Muslims believe in this theory. They believe that Jesus Christ was crucified but did not die on the cross. He was purely unconscious. They believe that Christ wandered around in Israel for forty days, after forty days he ran away to Kashmir and lived there till the age of 120. According to Ahmedia Muslims, Jesus Christ died there and was buried in Srinagar Kashmir. They also claim that, *"Christ's grave is in Mahala Khanyar Srinagar Kashmir."* [6]

To prove this, they say that Srinagar means place of Skull which is mentioned in the Bible and in Hebrew it is called Golgatha. In Kashmir there is one place called Gilgith. Al Haj Khwaja Nazir Ahmad has written that, *"Christ came to Kashmir twice, in his first journey he came via Syria, Afghanistan, Pakistan, Sri Lanka, India and*

Nepal to Kashmir." [7] *"In his second journey, Christ came to Kashmir via Iraq, Iran, Afghanistan and Pakistan."* [8]

Page 353 states *"Hazrat Isa left his mother in Israel and later she travelled with two other brothers to come and live with Hazrat Isa in Kashmir, but on the way, she died and was buried there. Still that place is known by her name Mari which is now changed to Murree. In Afghani and Kashmiri language, Mari is used for Mary. Her tomb is near the defence tower in Murree which is at the Pindi Point. The local people call it Mai Mari Da Asthan (Mother Mary's resting place)"* [9]

If Christ was crucified on the cross and he was not dead but was just unconscious, then the people of that time were foolish as they did not know the difference between a dead and an unconscious man or the soldiers who were on duty to kill the criminal were not properly trained and they let the criminal go without killing him? The soldiers knew that if they let the criminal go away then the authorities would kill them. Do you think the soldiers were foolish or Nicodemus and Joseph Armethia were foolish who buried Christ with 10 Kg of spices on his body? Could they not discern between a dead person and an unconscious one?

Second question, is that if he was alive and was just unconscious then we should not forget that his hands, feet, head, back and side were bleeding. He didn't receive any medical treatment for three days. His whole blood was drained out which meant the ultimate death. If we assume that he was not dead, then how can we believe that he started his journey from Jerusalem and ended up in Kashmir? If he safely arrived in Kashmir, lived there for 120 years then why did He refrain from preaching the gospel there? If Christ lived in Kashmir for 120 years and was well known all over the country then why did the Roman government not try to arrest Him and crucify Him all over again. Why did they not pursue Him and let their criminal go easily?

We see that Christ was 30 years old when he started his preaching ministry. He was 33 and a half years old when he was crucified on the cross. He only preached for three and half years and yet the multitude of followers that listened and embraced His teaching is staggering. But he was 33 and a half years old when he came to Kashmir and lived there for 120 years. In this way, he preached there for 87 years but could not convert even one single person. Perplexing? Or was it that when He came to Kashmir, He decided not to preach the gospel. So what was the reason that He could not win a single person for God? Could it be that His miracle working power had vanished? Or that He decided to abandon God and started living His life solo, independent of God?

If we accept that Christ did not die on the cross but was just unconscious and later He started his journey from Jerusalem and ended up in Kashmir, then this is a great miracle; a great miracle indeed! It is extraordinary that a frail and wounded person, like Jesus, could be so mobile and travel a great distance.

This being the case, we have another question to present: If Christ lived in Kashmir for 120 years, knowing that His disciples were being persecuted by the Romans, why did He not send relief to them? Or tell them to come to Kashmir and live with Him there? Why did He remain silent when his disciples and followers were being inhumanly persecuted? All these questions, encourage us to reject this interpretation that Christ did not die on the cross and instead came to Kashmir and lived there for 120 years.

Dr Sir James Simpson, an eminent medical expert, inventor of the chloroform to numb tissues. He wrote regarding the scientific proof of the death of Christ and about what eventually caused His death. He concluded that Christ died on the cross because His heart burst. He wrote that when someone dies with their arms out stretched and the individual shouting, these two physical activities inevitably causes the heart to burst. The reaction is that the heart gets filled with blood. The heart is then unable to pump it out quickly, as the person needs a lot of strength to pump out the blood; they then encounter difficulty in breathing. The end result is that the heart cannot beat and bursts as a result of the heavy blood pressure. Science now knows that blood remains in its original condition but shortly after death it separates into blood and water. The Bible teaches us that Jesus Christ died on the cross with a loud voice and soon after a soldier pierced His side, water and blood gushed out, which is a solid proof of His death.

Medically, science proves that Christ died because his heart was burst on the cross. The Bible accepts this proof because David prophesied about Christ in Psalm 69:20, *"Scorn has broken my heart and has left me helpless; I looked for sympathy, but there was none, for comforters, but I found none."* So all these witnesses, reveal that Christ really died on the cross.

Endnotes:

6. Al Haj Khwaja Nazir Ahmad, *'Jesus in heaven on earth,'* Azeez Manzil, Brandreth Road, Lahore, Pakistan, page 377

7. Al Haj Khwaja Nazir Ahmad, *'Jesus in heaven on earth,'* Azeez Manzil, Brandreth Road, Lahore, Pakistan, page 339

8. Al Haj Khwaja Nazir Ahmad, *'Jesus in heaven on earth,'* Azeez Manzil, Brandreth Road, Lahore, Pakistan, page 377

9. Al Haj Khwaja Nazir Ahmad, *'Jesus in heaven on earth,'* Azeez Manzil, Brandreth Road, Lahore, Pakistan, page 353

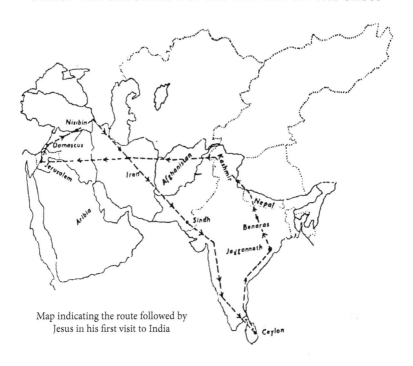

Map indicating the route followed by
Jesus in his first visit to India

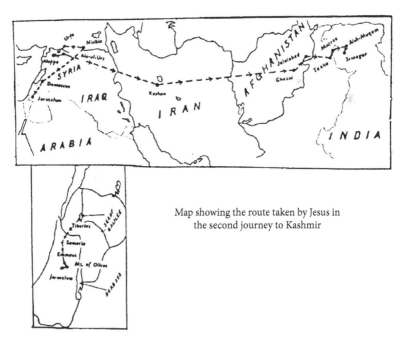

Map showing the route taken by Jesus in
the second journey to Kashmir

3.4 *Was Christ resurrected?*

It is true that Jesus Christ was crucified, died and buried but his body was stolen and because they could not find his body they thought that he had risen from the dead? This is what many Muslims say.

There are three different views about who stole the body of Christ:

FIRST VIEW:
The Disciples of Christ had stolen the body of Christ.

First of all, the Jews said that His disciples had stolen His body. Our minds does not accept this view that a few weak, scared and unorganized disciples can deceive the trained and equipped soldiers and can steal the dead body, without any disturbance. Scripture tells us that the disciples were petrified, their very lives were in danger and they were hiding in an upper room. How could they possibly even attempt to steal the body when they were trying to keep out of sight from the authorities and potential lynch mob?

In Matthew's Gospel, it is written that the soldiers came and told the full account of what had happened to the body.
Deceitfully, the chief priest bribed them and dictated to them that if anybody should enquire regarding the whereabouts of the body that they are to tell them that whilst they slept the disciples came and stole the body of Christ.

The question remains: How did they know that it was His disciples who had stolen the body of Christ? If they were awake then why did they not resist and stop them? And, the second question must also be addressed: They had broken protocol i.e. to sleep on duty was forbidden. It was an offence for a Roman soldier, who were fully trained and equipped to even sleep on duty.

Why was this overlooked or sanctioned? If we assume that they were tired so that is why they slept then how did they know that the people who stole the body of Christ were His disciples?

Another very serious question is if the disciples stole the body of Christ then why did they face persecution? Why did they proclaim that Christ had been raised from the dead and, they had seen Him? If all this was a lie then why were they willing to die or be killed for his name's sake? Why did they not tell the truth? They were stoned but they rejoiced. If it was all a lie, then why were their lives radically changed? Why did they develop steely hearts and turn the full course of their lives to live solely and according to the teaching of Christ? In this way, on the basis of all these details, we reject this first point of view.

SECOND VIEW:
This view argues that the Jews stole the body of Christ.

This is a completely baseless and senseless theory. We need to remember that the Jews crucified Christ on the cross and they put guardsmen on his grave so nobody could steal His body. So why would they steal from themselves?

So if we assume that the Jews stole the body of Christ, why is it when the disciples were preaching nationwide, fearlessly proclaiming that Jesus Christ, "has been risen from the dead" why did the Jews remain silent? Why did they not take the disciples to the place where His body was and tell them, "See here is the body of Christ?" In this way, this whole drama would have ended there. Then Christianity would not have grown and nobody would have followed the teachings of Christ. But that didn't happen. What followed then went down into church history: Christians faced persecution from the Romans and the Jews; Christians were thrown to hungry lions; they were mercilessly thrown into the fire; they were killed; they were stoned and yet they multiplied in number and began to take over the whole world. But none of the Jews presented the body of Christ; this was impossible because they couldn't do so. They simply did not have Christ's body. So this theory dies.

THIRD VIEW:
The body of Christ was relocated by Joseph of Armethia.

This blame is superficial by itself and has no strength because the Jews had appointed guards on the tomb to watch over Christ. If Joseph wanted to relocate the body of Christ, he had to take permission from the Roman authority and without their permission he was forbidden. If we assume that he took permission from the Roman authority than they knew the exact whereabouts of the body.

Another crucial factor overlooked, Joseph needed manpower to relocate the body of Christ, he simply could not achieve this objective all by himself, there was a hefty humungous rock in front of the tomb of Christ which he could not roll away by himself. If we assume that he got some help from others then why did these 'helpers' not disclose this secret and tell other people about the body of Christ. In this way, this whole drama could end just there. But the reality is that Jesus Christ was raised from the dead and so many people saw him after His resurrection.

"For what I received I pass on to you as of first importance; that Christ died for our sins according to the scriptures, that he was buried, that he was raised on the third day according to the scriptures, and that he appeared to Cephas, and then to the twelve. After that, he appeared to more than five hundred of the brothers and sisters at the same time, most of who are still living, though some have fallen asleep. Then he appeared to James, then to all the apostles, and last of all he appeared to me also, as to one abnormally born." (1 Corinthians 15:3-8)

The Apostle Paul said that Christ appeared to more than five hundred people and most of them were still alive at the time when Paul wrote his epistle to the Corinthians. If this was not true, they could challenge Paul and prove him wrong. He also says that Jesus appeared to the twelve apostles, James and lastly, to Paul himself. So we have so many witnesses of the resurrection. Thomas has cleared all our doubts.

"Now Thomas (also known as Didymus), one of the twelve, was not with the disciples when Jesus came. So the other disciples told him, "we have seen the Lord!" But he said to them, "unless I see the nail marks in his hands and put my finger where the nails were, and put my hand into his side, I will not believe." A week later his disciples were in the house again and Thomas was with them. Though the doors were locked, Jesus came and stood among them and said, "Peace be with you!" Then he said to Thomas, "put your finger here; see my hands. Reach out your hand and put it into my side. Stop doubting and believe." Thomas said to him, "my Lord and my God!" (John 20:24-28)

In this account we see that Thomas has completely dismissed any doubts about the resurrection of Jesus Christ. We confidently know for a fact that the person who was raised from the dead was our Lord Jesus Christ, who was hanged on the cross with nails, barbarically pounded into his hands and feet.

So all these witnesses prove that Jesus died on the cross, He was buried and on the third day, rose from the dead. For centuries, people have vehemently denied the resurrection of our Lord Jesus Christ; but until now, none has given any solid reason to prove that Christ did not rise from the dead. Numerous people continue to refuse the resurrection of Jesus because they do not want to abide by His teachings; out of rebellion or obstinacy they reject the spiritual principles He has set for their lives. If Christ has risen from the dead, according to His claims, then He is truly a supernatural person. With this knowledge, we can safely place our confidence in His words as He claimed to be divine and also the Saviour of the world. We need to believe this with every ounce of our mind, spirit and soul. So "everything that has breath" must acknowledge and surrender, follow and accept Him as their Messiah, Lord and Saviour. We must accept whole heartedly that Christ died on the cross for our sins and was raised from the dead to give us a new and eternal life.

3.5 *If Jesus is God, how can He, as God, die?*

Before we answer this question, we need to know what Christians believe about Jesus and the true nature of Jesus Christ.

As Christians we believe that Jesus is fully God and fully man. He has two natures: human and divine. When we say that Jesus is God, He is God in power and attributes. When we say that Jesus was human, this means that He had human feelings, emotions and needs like us to sleep but God cannot sleep. He used to eat and get hungry but God cannot get hungry. He used to get tired but God cannot get tired.

Within the one person of Christ, there are two distinct natures, divine and human. We see evidence of the divine attributes of Christ in the word of God:

"In the beginning was the word and the word was with God, and the word was God... and the word became flesh, and dwelt among us..."
(John 1:1, 14)

"Thomas answered and said to Him (Jesus), My Lord and my God!"
(John 20:28)

"For in him (Jesus) all the fullness of Deity dwells in bodily form."
(Colossians 2:9)

Jesus' own statement about himself that, *"I and the Father are one."* (John 10:30)

"Sacrifice and offering You did not desire, but a body You have prepared for Me." (Hebrews 10:5)

But when Jesus died on the cross, it was not His divine nature, as God, that died. It was His human nature that died. Dying is a biological function that is reserved only for human nature. God cannot die.

We see human attributes of humanity in Christ in the following way such as: He wept, He ate, He slept and He had a body. So we see humanity in the expression of his attributes physically.

Likewise, we see the divine nature of Christ through His human nature. We understand how the person of Christ exercised His divine attributes when He walked on water (Matthew 14:29), forgave sins (Luke 5:20), claimed to pre-exist with the Father (John 17:5) and said that He would be with the disciples always (Matthew 28:20).

So Jesus is both divine and human. He is both God and man. When we say that Jesus is God and that Jesus died on the cross, we are not saying that the God-nature died. Rather, we are saying the person of Christ with human nature died on the cross. Another way to understand this is to know the meaning of the word to 'die.' To die does not mean to just go out of existence. Even Muslims believe this, that's why they go to the sharians of the dead people and pray to them. Death is separation.

Physical death is when the soul-spirit separates from the physical body. So in this sense, yes, God died because Jesus was God in human form and Jesus' soul-spirit separated from His body.

However, if by death we mean 'a cessation of existence', then, no, God did not die. For God to 'die' in that sense would mean that He ceased to exist and neither the Father nor the Son nor the Holy

Spirit will ever cease to exist.

The Son, the second person of the Trinity, left the body and temporarily inhabited a body on earth because he said that God prepared a body for Him, but his divine nature as God did not die, nor could it die.

CHAPTER 4

Why trust the Bible?

When I came to know Jesus on 30th September 1994, my life was completely turned upside down and I wanted to tell everybody what Jesus had done for me. In January 1996, I read a book called 'God's Smugglers' written by Brother Andrew, founder of Open Doors, this book impacted my life greatly. Before I finished the book, God spoke to me that I too needed to do something similar to Brother Andrew and his bold exploits for the Kingdom of God. As I was reading the book, I felt that God's plan was slowly being revealed to me. When I finished the book I could not sleep for many nights; I was restless. Almost every night God was saying the same thing again and again, but I was not audacious enough to take the responsibility presented to me or it was that I simply did not know how to do what He was calling for me to do.

For two months I was in a state of unrest. During my turmoil I shared with friends what God was saying to me. One of my friends Sohail, agreed to join me in my venture. On 6th March 1996, with some spare money that I had, I made photocopies of a leaflet entitled: 'Four Things Which God Wants You to Know' and distributed them in the streets of Islamabad. After distributing these leaflets, the joy that God gave us was impossible to put into words. That was the beginning of 'Go and Save Islamabad' Ministry.

God blessed and multiplied this ministry and in a couple of years it turned into 'Go And Save Pakistan' and finally rested on 'Go And Save International.' Under this banner we started adult education schools, trained young leaders for Muslim evangelism and distributed the gospel to every single house in Islamabad three times over. The ministry was vibrant, all ages were involved: the young, the old, youth, men and women. In my country, it is not common for young girls and women to distribute literature but in 'Go And Save Pakistan', all went out. Many times we were arrested by the police, we were locked up in the police station, stoned, beaten, verbally abused but every time the joy of the Lord and mercy of the Lord was great and beyond our understanding. Praise, glory, thanks and honour to our God Father for everything He has done.

We have distributed more than 50,000 gospels of John's Gospel in Islamabad to almost every single house. During the distribution we faced so much persecution but we have so many amazing testimonies. A few of these I will share with you. Do also keep in mind that Pakistan is a Muslim country and giving Christian literature to Muslims is strictly prohibited.

During one occasion we were distributing the gospel according to John in Islamabad Zoo. There was a Muslim priest who tried to stone us and he encouraged other Muslims to follow suit.

Many Muslims gathered together to stone us. Whilst they were hurling stones at us, we started praying for them and none of us were bruised in anyway; they felt the supernatural power of God protecting us and abruptly stopped. Some of the Muslims escorted us safely out from the zoo.

Countless times we were arrested by the police and frequently beaten by them and other Muslim people. One particular time, when we were arrested, they took us to the police station and tortured us. During that time one of their officers came, he read the Gospel according to John, and found nothing inflammatory or blasphemous against Islam. God touched his heart and he released us and sternly warned us to discontinue our distribution to the Muslim community. Previously, they had seized all our literature. On our release we brazenly requested to take it back. Dutifully they returned all the literature and immediately we started distributing the tracts to the people who were in the police station. This is uncommon in Pakistan. When they arrest someone, they do not release them without money (a bribe) whether you have done something wrong or not. You have to pay the bribe; regardless. We paid nothing.

Another time, the police arrested us and when they took us to the police station and tortured us, we started praying for them loudly. We prayed that God would bless, protect and promote then in their job ranks. God touched their hearts, they released us and even took us right back to the same place where they had arrested us. This is very unusual!

On one such occasion, we were again distributing literature and unexpectedly heavy rain fell. We prayed that God would stop the rain until we finished our distribution. Immediately God stopped the rain. We continued with our distribution and once completed the rain again started instantly along with thunderstorms.

4.1 *Who wrote the Bible?*

The Bible is known as the mother of books. The English word Bible, is derived from a root designating the inner bark of the linden tree, on which the ancient people wrote their books, normally called Papyrus. Papyrus was called Biblus. Greek people used to call a big book Biblos and a small book Biblion.

In the second century, the Greek Christians started calling their holy scriptures Tabiblia, which means books. When this word came into the Latin language, they thought that it was a singular word Biblia and this same word Biblia translated into English as Bible, which we use today. The Bible is a living word. It is God's living word which has changed lives: the sinful nature of man and the evil thoughts of a man and gives him a new life, new thoughts and a new purpose of life.

The Bible consists of sixty-six books. These sixty-six books have been divided into two parts. The first part is called the Old Testament and the second part is called the New Testament. The Old Testament consists of 39 books and the New Testament consists of 27 books. The scripture which was written before Christ is called the Old Testament, in that part there is the old covenant which God made with his people on Mount Sinai. The scripture which was written after Christ is called the New Testament. In this section, there is a new covenant which was made with his people on Mount of Calvary. Both covenants complement each other.

The new covenant is hidden in the old covenant and the old covenant is revealed in the new covenant. You cannot separate these two covenants from each other; they are interwoven. If you try to understand these two covenants separately, you will not be able to understand it. These two covenants are one but are revealed in two different time periods.

Almost all the books of the Old Testament were written in the Hebrew language except Proverbs which was written in Greek. Ezra, Daniel and some parts of the book of Jeremiah were written in Aramaic language. The Bible was written by forty different writers, in three different languages, under different circumstances. Most of them were unknown to each other. They wrote at various periods during the space of about 1600 years and yet after all, it is only one book dealing with only one subject in its countless aspects and relations, the subject of man's redemption.

These writers came from every social rank of society: Moses was a shepherd but he learnt all the wisdom of Egypt; Joshua was a soldier and a spy; Ezra was a renowned accountant and faithful priest; Nehemiah was the king's cupbearer; David was a shepherd, a musician, warrior and a great king; Solomon was the most intelligent person who ever walked the earth and nevertheless was a very powerful king; Isaiah was a prophet; Ezekiel was a Jewish slave; Daniel was a great politician; Amos was a shepherd and farmer; Matthew was a tax collector; Peter and John were fishermen and uneducated; Luke was a doctor and Paul was a tent maker and yet, a highly educated person. They all were very diverse from each other.

The Bible is God's own word. The Bible mentions more than two hundred times that the *"Lord says."*
One of the Bible's unique attributes is that it does not favour anyone. No one can correct it. This is God's own word which was written by the power of the Holy Spirit. This is inspired by God. This is the breath of God.

4.2 *Is the Bible reliable, or an untrustworthy and corrupt book?*

No other book in the history of the world has been criticized, analysed or scrutinised more meticulously than the Bible.

Many people who are anti-Christian have worked tirelessly to attempt to extinguish the Bible since its inception but have failed miserably. Many countries have taken a bold stand to even ban it altogether. Countless numbers of people have sacrificed their very lives to protect the Holy Scriptures. They have refused to live in a world without God's sacred word. Innumerable rulers throughout the ages have worked relentlessly, uncompromisingly to extinguish God's word; they have burnt countless copies but to no avail. In their feeble attempts to prove that this is an untrustworthy and corrupt book, they have encountered disappointment time and time again.

The vindictive, premeditated manner in which men have violently opposed the Bible, had it been any other manuscript it would have been destroyed entirely by now; non-existent. Still, this book is the most widely read in the world. All over the earth, the Bible is the most treasured book throughout the ages. In every direction of life, people read; follow its instructions with all their heart, mind and spirit. This book has been translated into more than 2,300 languages. Now almost 96% of people in the world can read or listen to the Bible in their mother tongue.

All translation is comprehensive primarily because the original language of this book is very easy and simple as well. This book is equally loved by the rich, the poor, kings and scholars, the wise, the foolish the strong and the weak. It has been a blessing to individuals, people groups, families, communities and whole nations.

The Bible talks about God's plan, man's sinful nature, the way and joy of salvation, the consequences of sin, eternal life and the everlasting kingdom of God. The history of this book is true, the teachings of this book are holy, the law is acceptable, and the decision is unchangeable. There is light for the person sitting in darkness. Authority is released through this book; there is wisdom in this book for the ignorant; holiness for believers and faith for the weak. Now we will see how archaeology, science and history proves this witness/evidence.

Scientific Proof:
The purpose of the Bible is not to give us scientific information

but when it talks about scientific matters it is precise. Science verifies what the Bible declares. Here are some examples:

- There is weight in the wind. Job 28:25
- The earth was formed out of water and by water. 2 Peter 2:3
- The earth is round. Isaiah 40:22
- The earth hangs on nothing. Job 25:5

The Bible according to its medical revelation is an unique book. Moses said to the Israelites that they can eat the animals who have a divided hoof and that chew the cud. They are clean. However, of those that chew the cud or that have a divided hoof you may not eat for example the camel. They are unclean for you. (Deuteronomy 14:1-7)

Modern science has demonstrated that animals like rabbits, camels and pigs have a distinct kind of bacteria which continues to live even when cooked on a very high temperature, which could probably become the cause of many diseases within the human body. The Bible also forbids us to eat dead animals (Deuteronomy 14:21) because when the animals dies the bacteria level in their bodies increases quicker which becomes the cause of spreading different disease.

Jesus predicted His second coming, saying that when He returns it will be both night and day (Luke 17:31-34). Such a passage has baffled many over time, that on Christ's return it will be both 'night and day' at the same time. Now we know that in some parts of the world it is day in another part of the world is it is night. These are some of the examples from the Bible which proves that it is exact in its claims and sayings. Science has verified time and time again thousands of claims of the Bible which encourages us to believe that this book is not by human efforts but is the breath of God.

Archaeological Proof:
Archaeology has given us much historical proof pertaining to the authenticity and claims of the Bible. W.F. Albright, an eminent archaeologist, has commented about the Old Testament that, *"No doubt, the study of archaeology has revealed the historian evidence of the Old Testament. Hittite people or nation has been mentioned sixty-six times in the Old Testament. People did not believe anything about these statements which were made about the Hittites. People thought that it is fiction because we don't find any account in the historical books or writing about the Hittite people. Because of lack of evidence, some scholars thought that there was no such nation or people on this earth. But now modern studies have proved that the Hittites were a civilisation of that time. Archaeology has found hundreds of Hittite tablets, ideals and paintings on the Hittite people in modern Turkey. When they dug in Bogazkoy, they found 1300 mud tablets which were in the Hittite language and by these tablets, very easily; we can know their culture and history."* [10]

Another biblical account which was greatly targeted by secular scholars was the defeat of Jericho City. When Joshua and the Israelites reached near the city, God gave them very unusual instructions. He told them to march around the city for six days once each time, but on the seventh day God told them to march around the city seven times and on the seventh time God commanded them to shout loudly and to blow the trumpet. Following God's command, the walls of Jericho city fell. Joshua and his army entered into the city and conquered it. God instructed them not to take anything from the city, but to burn it to the ground as it says in Joshua 6.

"Professor Garius Tang started digging this area 1930 to 1937. When they dug this area, they were amazed to know that the whole city was burned down without taking away anything from the city. They found so many burned things like wheat, flour dough and other grains. If the city was attacked from the outside, the wall must fall down towards inside but the professor was amazed to know that the city wall which

was ten feet wide and fifteen feet tall fell down towards outside and the invaders entered the city very easily by these walls." [11]

Recently archaeologists have dug in the Ur of the Chaldeans. They have revealed that a strong kingdom existed three to four thousand years before Christ. Their language was in parts similar to the Turkish language. In the ancient language of Mesopotamia or Babylon is known as Eden. They used to worship one god but later on they started worshipping many gods made of wood and stone. *They used to call themselves 'sons of God' and to outsiders 'Sons of the man.'* [12] This discovery helps us to understand Genesis 6:2 which say that, *"the sons of God saw that the daughters of man were beautiful, and they married any of them they chose."* This reveals that the men of Ur of the Chaldeans were married to the women of Eden.

"Sir Flanders Pateri found a weapon during his research in Gaza which was like the shape of the jaw of the horse or donkey. The teeth of this weapon were very sharp. Sir Flanders Pateri says that it was a very powerful and useful weapon. This same kind of weapon was used by Samson in the book of Judges 15:15-16." [13]

Modern archaeologists have dug in ancient Jerusalem, Samaria and different parts of Canaan and discovered so many valuable things which not only highlight the books of the Jewish Scripture like the first and second book of Samuel, first and second book of Kings and the first and second books of Chronicles and amazingly proved it as well. Archaeological records come out of their graves and loudly shout that all the writings which were written between fourteenth century to 485BC were 100% accurate. *"Professor Aaligaro writes that hardly there is any single day which does not reveal the truth of the biblical scriptures."* [14]

The Manuscripts of the Bible:

Many people have asked how ancient manuscripts were written and preserved over time. Modern study of archaeology has made it very easy to know the answer. *"In early days, Egyptians used to write on papyrus. Papyrus was a plant which used to grow beside the banks of river Nile. Ancient people used to collect the leaf of papyrus and used to join them in a row and used to make a scroll which was usually 15 to 20 feet long. They used to write on the scroll and used to save it in the jar of mud."* [15] Canaanites used to write on the mud tablets with the sharp edge of the metal and then used to cook it in the fire to preserve it.

The Hebrews used to write on different things over the ages such as mud tablets, animal skins and papyrus. There are more than two thousand manuscripts of the Hebrew Holy Scriptures. These manuscripts are written on different objects and found in different conditions. Some scripts are in immaculate condition whilst others are in very poor condition. Some scripts are challenging to read and some appear as if they had been written recently. Such manuscripts have been found from the different parts of the world like the land of Canaan, Babylon, South Asia, Africa, Europe and China. All these manuscript of the Bible are the same, word by word.

Now let us talk about the manuscripts of the New Testament. The gospels and the different parts of the New Testament which has been found in the original Greek language are more than five thousand. The scripts of the gospels in Latin translation, which are called vulgate, more than five thousand copies have been rescued. More than one thousand copies of the Syrian and Aramaic translated manuscripts have been found. That means now we have more than fourteen thousand manuscripts of the gospels to know the original script of the gospels. Is there any wise person in this world who can deny finding the actual word of the gospels?

The witness of the Quran:
The Quran states that the Jews are rebellious and disloyal to their God. However, the Quran never dishonours their Holy Scriptures. Muhammad also gave honour and respect to their Holy Scripture.

He respected all the prophets of the Old Testament and was reverential when discussing their Holy Scriptures.

Now we will see what the Quran states about the Jewish Holy Scriptures.

"Indeed, we sent down the Torah, in which was guidance and light. The prophets who submitted judged by it for the Jews, as did the rabbis and scholars by that which they were entrusted of the scripture of Allah, and they were witnesses there to." (Surah Al Maidah 5:45)

"And we sent, following in their footsteps, Jesus, the son of Mary, confirming that which came before him in the Torah; and we gave him the Gospel, in which were guidance and light and confirming that which came before it of the Torah as guidance and instruction for the righteous." (Surah Al Maidah 5:46)

"O you have believed, believed in Allah and His messenger and the book that He sent down upon His messenger and the scriptures which he sent down before. And whoever disbelieves in Allah, His angels, His books, His messengers and the last day has certainly gone for astray." (Surah Al Nisa 4:136)

"And we sent not before you except men to whom we revealed. So ask the people of the Scripture if you do not know." (Surah Al Nahl 16:43)

"So if you are in doubt, (O Muhammad), about that which we have revealed to you, then ask those who have been reading the Book before you." (Surah Al Yunus 10:94)

These verses help us to know that the Quran fully trusts the accuracy and authenticity of the Bible. It encourages Muhammad and other Muslims that if you have any doubt about any religious or spiritual matters then you are to go to the people of the book i.e. Jews and Christians.

In the first passage, we see that there is light and guidance for the people in the Torah. In the second passage, we saw that there is light, guidance and instruction for the righteous in the Gospel. The third passage clearly instructs Muslims to believe in the Gospel and the Torah and if they do not believe it, then they certainly will go astray. Numerous times, when we talk to Muslims, they openly declare that they believe in the Bible but they do not need to read it. Once a Muslim man said to me the same thing and then I told him the difference between "knowing and believing." I told him that I knew that he believed that Muhammad was the last messenger of Allah, according to his faith, and that he entered the world and in doing so Allah gave him the Quran. So you believe in Muhammad and the Quran, that's why you read the Quran and follow the teaching of Muhammad. But I don't believe in Muhammad or the Quran that's why I don't read the Quran and don't follow the teaching of Muhammad.

If I believe and follow the teaching of Muhammad and Quran then I am not a Christian but a Muslim. But you believe in the Bible and all the prophets of the Old Testament but you don't follow the teaching of other prophets and don't read the Bible. Then what kind of faith is this? If Muslims believe in the Bible then they need to read it and follow the teachings of the book as well; as we Christians believe in the Old Testament and we read it and follow its teachings. For this reason, if Muslims believe in the Bible, they need to read it as instructed.

The fourth passage shows Allah instructing Muhammad that if he fails to comprehend matters then he needs to go back to the people of the book, i.e. Jews and Christians. So on the basis of these Quranic verses, we can confidently conclude that the Bible is not only an accurate book but one of authenticity that we can entirely trust. This book is the same consistent manuscript as it was thousands of years ago. Nations rise and vanish; languages come and go; kings exalt themselves but soon fade; the things of this world change rapidly with today's fad becoming tomorrow's history but the Bible, the infallible Bible is the same and will remain unchangeable to the end of this world. So that is why I want to encourage you to believe that the Bible is a trustworthy and an incorruptible living book. You can read it confidently knowing that it directs you to eternal life; it declares freedom from bondage of sin and how to be free from the captivity of Satan and this book gives you a glimpse of heaven.

Endnotes:

10. Wiclif-A Singh, 'The authenticity of the Bible,' M.I.K, 36 Ferozpur Road, Lahore, page 218.

11. Wiclif-A Singh, 'The authenticity of the Bible,' M.I.K, 36 Ferozepur Road, Lahore, Pakistan, page 227.

12. Arch-Decon Barkat Ullah, 'Proofs of the biblical books,' M.I.K, 36 Ferozepur Road, Lahore, page 70-73.

13. Arch-Decon Barkat Ullah, 'Proofs of the biblical books,' M.I.K, 36 Ferozepur Road, Lahore, page 79.

14. Arch-Decon Barkat Ullah, 'Proofs of the biblical books,' M.I.K, 36 Ferozepur Road, Lahore, page 71

15. Yousaf Masih Yaad, 'The greatness of Al-Kitab,' Christian Writers, Peshawar, page 60.

4.3 Is the Bible that we have today still unchanged, or has it been altered?

First of all, we need to know what it means to say that the 'content' of the Bible had been changed. Does it mean that someone has knowingly and purposefully taken out parts of the Bible i.e. verses and added things which were not part of the Bible? If this is the case, then we need to know the answers to these questions. When was it changed? Why was it changed? Who changed it? Which parts of the Bible have been changed and where in the world was it changed?

Every Christian or non-Christian scholar who sincerely researched the Word of God has found that the content of the Bible is the same as it was at the time of writing. This is an unrealistic remark! Jewish people used to give the great honour and paramount reverence to their Holy Scripture. They used to duplicate their scriptures with meticulous care arising from a sincere heart, complete faithfulness, and industrious effort and with a fear of the Lord.

At the forefront of their minds was accuracy. Accuracy coupled without a single mistake. The scribes had special instructions that ordered them to write each word before reading it. To make an error was forbidden or impossible. Before they wrote the name of God, they were required to pray and wash their pen. Especially when they had to write the name 'Yahweh' (the holiest name of God), they were required to wash their whole body and then had to put on complete Jewish clothing.

Every book of the Scripture, they used to re-examine within the fifteen says of the completion. If they found two or more mistakes in the script, they use to bury it into the land.

"The council of Jamnia which was held in late first century decided how to write the Jewish Scripture. In this council they decided that how many words will be in each line of the book. How many lines will be on each page? They decided that how much space they have to give between two words. They decided that which kind of ink and colour of the ink, they will use for the writing of their scriptures. Even they decided in the council that what kind of dresses scribes have to put on when they will write the Scripture. They decided special instructions for the scribes when they will copy the Scripture because every single word was God's own word." [16]

"Hebrew scribes who were ordained to copy the Scripture were very faithful and God fearing people. They counted every single word of each book. They counted every single word of the Bible and that how many times it has appeared in the Bible. For example, A (Alef) the first Hebrew alphabet has been used in the Bible forty-two thousand, three hundred and seventy-seven times (42,377). Second alphabet B (Bet) is used thirty-five thousand, two hundred and eighteen times (35,218). They tried their best to preserve the actual word of the Scripture which was used at the time of writing." [17]

By these examples, you can see that when the Jewish scribes wrote their scriptures, the bespoke care devoted as well as the honour and respect they gave was accompanied with great reverence and awe.

1) If we assume that the content of the Bible was changed before the Quran then Muslim people will encounter difficulties by themselves, because the Quran has instructed Muhammad that if he has any doubt about anything, he needs to consult with the people of the book who are Christians and Jews.

"Even the Quran also says that nobody can change the content of the word of God." (Surah Al-Hijr 15:9)

"Indeed, it is we who sent down the book and indeed, we will be its guardian." (Surah Yunus 10:64).

"For there are good tidings in the worldly life and in the hereafter. No change is there in the word of Allah. That is what the great attainment is." (Surah Al-Fath 48:23)

"(This is) the established way of Allah which has occurred before. And never will you find in the way of Allah any change."

All these verses are promises of Allah that no one can change the word of God. He has sent it and he will protect it.

2) If someone says that the content of the Bible has been changed after the Quran then very easily, we can validate it because we have more than 1600 years old manuscripts of the Bible and with the help of the scripts very quickly we can find out the original script of the Bible. On the basis of all these scripts which have been discovered by archaeologists from the different parts of the world, very easily we can create a new script of the original Bible. The Bible which we have in our hands now is very similar to the scripts which have been found from different parts of the world.

3) If someone argues that the content of the Bible has been changed by the Jews after the crucifixion of our Lord Jesus Christ, then the accuser will encounter great difficulty. Why did Christians worldwide remain silent? Why was there no mass international protest? History does not give us any kind of single sign that Jews tried or changed their holy scriptures.

4) Again, if someone states that the content of the Bible has been changed by the Christians then the Jews all over the world will not sit silent and they will not allow any other to change their holy scriptures. We don't see any evidence in the history that the Christians tried or changed the Scripture of the Jews.

5) If someone says that the content of the Bible has been changed by the Christians and Jews collectively, than the accuser will be called crazy because history shows that never ever have Christians and Jews been together. Since the establishment of Christianity, the Jews have rejected Christians. All over the world the Jews dislike and dishonour Christians. Even Jews do not accept Christ as their Messiah, then how can they change their scriptures with

the 'collaboration' of the Christians?

So we can boldly state that nobody has changed the word of God and this is a false accusation. The Bible which we have in our hands is one hundred percent accurate, trustworthy, reliable and incorruptible. If until now, someone does not believe, then this accusation is of his own creation. He/she is a liar, a charlatan and simply a false accuser. They have no solid foundation to accuse. They cannot prove that the content of the Bible has been changed. If they continue in their disbelief then we will ask them to bring the original script and we will start reading that one. If he cannot bring the original script than the only option left is for them to accept the Bible which we have in our hands as original.

Endnotes:

16. Arch-Decon Barkat Ullah, '*Accuracy of the books of the Bible*,' MIK, 36 Ferozepur Road, Lahore, page 146.

17. Dr K L Nasir, '*Mother of Books*,' Faith Theological Seminary Gujranwala, Pakistan, page 147.

4.4 *Why are there four gospels in the New Testament?*

Many Muslims frequently ask this question: "We have only one Quran so why do you Christians have four gospels?" Christians do not believe in four gospels but in one gospel of our Lord Jesus Christ. There are no four gospels in the New Testament but one gospel which has been written by four different people by the inspiration of the Holy Spirit. These four writers have highlighted the four qualities of our Lord Jesus Christ. Their teaching is alike and talks about the different aspects of the life of Jesus Christ. These four gospel accounts support each other.

MATTHEW:

The Gospel according to Matthew presents Jesus Christ as the King of the Jews. Matthew quotes countless Old Testament prophecies and proves that Jesus is the promised King of the Jews. Matthew emphasises that Jesus came to fulfil all the prophecies of the Old Testament. He reveals how God made a plan for the salvation of all mankind, this started from Adam. He chose a nation for Him and then accomplished it through our Lord Jesus Christ. Matthew quotes from the 39 books of the Old Testament. There are 1,064 verses in this gospel and 644 verses are Jesus' own words. It means that one third of the gospel is Jesus' own words.

MARK:

The Gospel according to Mark presents Jesus as the Servant of God. Mark emphasises more on the miracles of Jesus Christ i.e. how he healed the sick, cast out demons and raised the dead.

LUKE:

The Gospel according to Luke presents Jesus as the Son of Man who is strong and mighty but filled with love, mercy and compassion. Luke discusses the human qualities of our Lord Jesus Christ. For example, he talks more about the prayer life of Jesus Christ more than any other of the gospel writers. Luke emphasises the reality that Jesus is the only Saviour of this world. Jesus offers salvation and forgiveness of sin to mankind regardless of their colour, race, gender or social status. He also emphasises that Jesus has power and authority to heal our body, spirit and soul. Luke highlights the great love and compassion of Jesus Christ for the underprivileged, women, the persecuted and those marginalised by society.

JOHN:

The Gospel according to John presents Jesus as the Son of God. John talks about His power and authority: how He raised the dead by a single command; he tells the story of Jesus commanding the dead man to come out from the grave, the dead man emerging and how He commanded the storm to stop and it stopped instantly. John emphasises the purpose of writing the gospel that people receive life and the abundant life by the name of Jesus Christ. *"But these are written that you might believe that Jesus is the Christ, the son of God; and that believing you might have life through his name."* (John 20:31)

These four gospels are written by the inspiration of the Holy Spirit and shows that they reveal the true identity and mission of Jesus Christ. Through these four gospels, we are able to know Christ's four aspects of his life and character. If there was only one gospel account, we would not be able to know the other three aspects of the life of Jesus Christ.

CHAPTER 5

Why not trust the Quran?

A female brethren from our church 'Z' worked as a cleaner, in the house of a diplomat. Working alongside her was a Muslim man who worked as the cook. One day, the Muslim man's wife came in crying. 'Z' asked her why she was upset. The Muslim man's wife told her that their daughter 'is possessed' and she continued to tell her that they had taken her to many Muslim priests but nobody could cure her.

One particular day they had taken her to the Muslim shrine, called Bari Amaam, in Islamabad. The Muslim priest, who was present, told them that they will have to cut her finger tips off her hands and feet and then her deliverance will come. This Muslim lady cried at the thought because not only will her daughter be disabled but will never be a bride. The daughter was severely violent and would only eat raw meat. She used to bite their buffalos, goats and other family members if they did not give her raw meat to eat. So they use to keep her in chains.

'Z' listened intently and replied,

"You don't need to cut the finger tips of your daughter."

She suggested that they should try a Christian priest and told them about our ministry. They invited us into their home. We went as a team and proceeded to pray for the girl. God delivered her on the same day. She is still healed and is now married and has a son. Praise, glory and honour to God!

5.1 *Scientific and Historical problems in the Quran*

Adam was made 90 feet tall.
The Prophet said, *"Allah created Adam, making him 60 cubits tall. When he created him, he said to him, "Go and greet that group of Angels and listen to their reply..."*
(Sahih Bukhari, book 55, Hadith 543, narrated by Abu Huraira)

The Hadith, which is the deeds and sayings of Muhammad are very important in Islam. Generally, a cubit is 18 inches. Therefore, Adam was 90 feet tall. It is physiologically impossible for a human to be 90 feet tall. The heart cannot pump enough blood around against the force of gravity for such a thing to be possible.

The soul exits through the collar-bone when leaving the body.
"Yea, when (the soul) reaches to the collar-bone (in its exits), and there will be a cry, who is a magician (to restore him)? And he will conclude that it was (the time) of parting. The sun set in murky water."
(Quran 75:26-28)

"Until, when he reaches the setting of the sun, he found it set in a spring of murky water: Near it he found a people: We said, O Zulqarnain! (You has authority) either to punish them, or to treat them with kindness."
(Quran 18:86)

Sperm comes from the chest of a man.
"Now let man but think from what he is created! He is created from a

drop emitted-proceeded from between the backbone and the ribs."
(Quran 86:5-7)

Shooting stars are for driving away evil spirits.
"And we have, (from of old), adorned the lowest heaven with lamps, and we have made such (lamps) (as) missiles to drive away the evil ones, and have prepared for them the penalty of the blazing fire." (Quran 67:5)

Crucifixion before it was invented.
"Pharaoh said, you believe in him before I give you leave! Lo! This is the plot that you have plotted in the city that you may drive its people hence. But you shall come to know! Surely I shall have your hands and feet cut off upon alternate sides. Then I shall crucify you every one."
(Quran 7:123-124)

Crucifixion was not invented until around 600BC by the Phoenicians. The Egyptians didn't crucify anyone because it had not been invented yet.

Mary (Mother of Jesus) is the sister of Aaron and Moses.
"Then she brought him to her own folk, carrying him. They said: O Mary! You have come with an amazing thing. O sister of Aaron! Your father was not a wicked man nor was your mother a harlot." (Quran 19:27-28)

Mary was not the sister of Aaron. Aaron was Moses' brother who lived many hundreds of years before Mary.

Passing wind while praying is sin.
"Allah's apostle said, the Angels keep on asking Allah's forgiveness for anyone of you, as long as he is at his Mu,Salla (praying place) and he doesn't pass wind. They say, "O Allah! Forgive him, O Allah! Be merciful to him."
(Sahih Bukhari, Hadith 436, vol.1, book 8, narrated by Abu Huraira)

A man slept through prayer time and the devil peed in his ear.
"It was mentioned before the prophet that there was a man who slept the night till morning (after sunrise). The Prophet said, "he is a man in whose ears Satan had urinated."
(Sahih Bukhari, Hadith 492, vol.4, book 54, narrated by Abdullah)

Muhammad ordered to drink camel urine.
"Some people from the tribe of ukl came to the prophet and embraced Islam. The climate of Medina did not suit them, so the prophet ordered them to go to the camels of charity and to drink their milk and urine."
(Hadith 794, vol.8, book 82, narrated by Anas)

Magic worked on Muhammad.
"Magic was worked on the prophet so that he began to fancy that he was doing a thing which he was not actually doing."
(Sahih Bukhari, Hadith 490, vol. 4, book 54. Narrated by Aisha)

How can that be if he was a prophet?

Muhammad acknowledged that he was a sinner.
The Prophet said, "I say "O Allah! Set me apart from my sins as the East and West are set apart from each other and clear me from sins as a white garment is cleaned of dirt. O Allah! Wash off my sins with water, snow and hail."
(Sahih Bukhari, Hadith 711, vol. 1, book 12, narrated by Abu Huraira.)

Muhammad taught that lying is okay.
"Muhammad bin Maslama got up saying, "O Allah's apostle! Would you like that I kill him (Kab bin al-Ashraf)? The Prophet said, yes, Muhammad bin Maslama said, and then allow me to speak a lie (to deceive Kab). The Prophet said, you may say it."
(Sahih Bukhari, Hadith 369, vol. 5, book 59)

It is okay to beat wives.
"As to those women on whose part you fear disloyalty and ill-conduct, admonish them (first), (next), refuse to share their beds, (And last) beat them." (Quran 4:34)

Temporary marriage allowed.
"Ibn Uray rerecorded: Ali reported that Jibir B. Abdullah came to perform Umra, and we came to his abode, and the people asked him about different things, and then they made a mention of temporary marriage, whereupon he said: yes, we had been benefiting ourselves by this temporary marriage during the life-time of the holy prophet and during the time of Abu Bakr and Umar." (Sahih Muslim, book 8, Hadith 3248)

Every new born baby is pricked by Satan and he cries from the touch of Satan.
"Abu Huraira reported: the messenger of Allah, peace and blessings is upon him, said, "No person is born but that he is pricked by Satan and he cries from the touch of Satan, except for Mary and her son (Isa)."
(Sahih Bukhari, 3248, Sahih Muslim 2366)

No repentance on one's deathbed.
"But repentance is not (accepted) of those who (continue to) do evil deeds up until, when death comes to one of them, he says, "indeed, I have repented now, or of those who die while they are disbelieves (the person who do not believe in Allah and last Prophet Muhammad). For them we have prepared painful punishment." (Quran 4:18)

Salvation is by good deeds.
"Then when the trumpet is blown, there will be no more relationships between them that Day, nor will one ask after another! Then those whose balance (of good deeds) is heavy, they will attain salvation: but those, whose balance is light, will be those who have lost their souls, in hell will they abide." (Quran 23:101-103)

The moon was split into two by Muhammad.
Muhammad split the moon into two pieces and this is one of the miracles which he performed.

"The hour has come near, and the moon has split (in two). And if they see a miracle, they turn away and say, "passing magic."
(Quran 54:1-2)

In 2010 a NASA Lunar Science Staff scientist named Brad Bailey said, "No current scientific evidence reports that the moon was split into two (or more) parts and then reassembled at any point in the past."

CHAPTER 6

Is Islam a religion of peace?

Muslims plotted to burn us alive!

Some years ago a friend and I were evangelising to a shopkeeper in Lodharian, near Bahawalpur, in Pakistan. The more we preached the angrier the shopkeeper became. After a short while, he began shouting and soon became inflamed. His fury spilled out and quite quickly began to gather a growing crowd. The shopkeeper, now having an audience, angrily informed them that we were evangelising to him and trying to convert him to Christianity. The entire crowd, whipped up into a mad, furious frenzy became enraged and started to beat and verbally abuse us. They then locked us up in the shop as they plotted what to do with us. After agreeing on their action, they later flung open the door and proceeded to frogmarch us to the main cross road with the intended aim to burn us alive.

However, a very handsome, well spoken man came and enquired what was happening. Members of the crowd told him that we were evangelising to the Muslim shopkeeper and what our present fate was. Listening intently the gentleman intervened and asked the crowd to stop procedures. He added that they used to go to Europe to evangelise to Europeans and the Europeans never reacted in such a violent manner. He concluded, "If you don't want to listen to them, don't listen but let them go." When the gentleman talked to the crowd, they were divided; one half wanted to burn us alive while the latter wanted to release us. Standing nervously on the road, with half the crowd screaming, "Allah wahakbar" (Allah is great), one of them turned to us and said, "Go and run away!" Immediately we did just that. Nobody, to our utter amazement, pursued us. In this way God saved our lives. I sincerely believe, that the well turned-out, gentleman who intervened and reasoned with the crowd, was Jesus. Praise God.

Bilal was killed by his Father
Bilal, was a recent Muslim convert. At age 24 years of age, he was truly a great seeker and was on fire for God. Almost every week, he would beg, "Baptize me!" He relentlessly asked each time when his baptism would be and then, he would conclude, "The Spirit of the Lord will come upon me like a dove." We baptised him in the Rawal Lake, in Islamabad. He was growing in the Lord but one day his family found his Bible which he kept hidden under his mattress. They were still unaware of his conversion. When his family confronted him regarding the Bible, he openly confessed that he had converted to Christianity and was also baptised in water. Sadly, his father, a police officer, shot him dead. The family said that he had committed suicide.

Amina's story: (Name and place has been charged)
A girl called Amina, was a Christian believer, she shared her faith with a Muslim girl called Hajira, who later became a Christian. Amina discipled Hajira. Hajira's family came to know that she had converted to Christanity. Hajira's three brothers, along with several other men, attacked Amina's house. They viciously beat Amina's father, breaking three ribs. Her brother and mother managed to escape. The men took Amina to an unidentified place, where each man raped her continuously for three days, after three

days they then took her to the police station. Whilst at the police station, she was yet again raped by the police officers. She was unable to give the exact number of how many police men had raped her. When the news became public, liberation came from a human rights NGO (Non Government Organisation) group, they rescued Amina. Sadly, I do not know where she is or what has happened to her.

Many people firmly state that Islam is a religion of peace. They believe that we worship the same God. Many people do not believe that the Quran and Hadith have violent passages or that both encourage violence. The question remains: If Islam is a religion of peace then why is there no peace in Muslim countries? Not only the Muslim countries but the Muslim majority areas of the world like Pakistan, Kashmir, Afghanistan, Iran, Iraq, Lebanon, Nigeria, South Sudan, Somalia, Algeria, Albania, Tajikistan, and so many other countries with Muslim strongholds?

Many Muslims blame other superpower countries for the wars in their nation, without accepting their own fault, or looking within. Muslim claims that Islam is a religion of peace; can you see peace in any part of the world wherever Muslims are in the majority? Do you know what the reason is? The reason is the teaching from the Quran and the Hadith that pertains to violence; both the Quran and Hadith actively encourage violence. Wherever Muslims are not submissive and they are creating problems, they are not living in peace like in China, the Philippines, Kashmir, Africa, Europe, and Australia. Have you thought about it, why they are not living in peace and why they cannot live peacefully alongside other religions and people groups? Muslims are not living in peace with Christians; they are not living in peace with Jews; they are not living in peace with Sikhs; they are not living in peace with Hindus; they are not living in peace with Buddhists and even Muslims are not living in peace with other Muslims all over the world.

So what is wrong with Islam? If Islam is a religion of peace then why are they not living in peace? This is an oxymoron. The latest writings of the Quran are the most violent. The Quran, in its late Medina-based texts, calls death to those who are not Muslim and even more to any person who decides to convert to another religion or simply put: 'stops being a Muslim.'

There is quite a huge disparity between a Muslim and Islam. Many Muslims as individuals, are peaceful and peace-loving because they do not know or follow Islam. But Islam is not a religion of peace. The Quran, Hadith, Islamic history and the present-day Muslim nations speak about the violence, so let the Quran speak up for itself.

6.1 *Violence in the Quran*

Below are some of the violent texts found in the Quran. They are sources of inspiration for the ongoing battles that are occurring in so many countries. Some may debate the actual intention and contexts of these texts. I will simply list them:

- Quran 2:191 – *"Slay the unbelievers wherever you find them."*
- Quran 3:28 – *"Muslims must not take the infidels as friend."*
- Quran 3:85 – *"Any religion other than Islam is not acceptable."*
- Quran 5:33 – *"Maim and crucify infidels if they criticise Islam."*
- Quran 8:12 – *"Terrorise and behead those who believe in scriptures other than the Quran."*
- Quran 8:60 – *"Muslims must muster all weapons to terrorise the infidels."*
- Quran 8:65 – *"The unbelievers are stupid; urge the Muslims to fight them."*

116

- Quran 9:5 - *"When opportunities arise, kill the infidels wherever you catch them."*
- Quran 9:30 - *"The Jews and the Christians are perverts; fight them."*
- Quran 9:123 - *"Make war on the infidels living in your neighbourhood."*
- Quran 22:19 - *"Punish the unbelievers with garments of fire, hooked iron rods, boiling water; melt their skin and bellies."*
- Quran 47:4 - *"Do not hanker for peace with the infidels; behead them when you catch them."*

"Fight them so that there will be no disbelief in Allah and Allah's religion will become dominant." (Quran 2:193)

"And if you are killed in the cause of Allah or die-then forgiveness from Allah and mercy are better than whatever they accumulate (in this world)." (Quran 3:157)

"So let those fight in the cause of Allah who sell the life of this world for the Hereafter. And he who fights in the cause of Allah and is killed or achieves victory-we will bestow upon him a great reward." (Quran 4:74)

O you, who have believed, do not take the Jews and the Christians as friends. They are (infect) friends of one another. And whoever is a friend to them among you-then indeed, he is (one) of them. Indeed, Allah guides not the wrongdoing people." (Quran 5:51)

"And you didn't kill them, but it was Allah who killed them. And you threw not (O Muhammad), when you threw, but it was Allah who threw that he might test the believers with a good test. Indeed, Allah is hearing and knowing." (Quran 8:17)

"Fight them, Allah will punish them by your hands and will disgrace them and give you victory over them and satisfy the breasts of a believing people." (Quran 9:14)

"O you who have believed, what is (the matter) with you that, when you are told to go forth in the cause of Allah, you adhere heavily to the earth? Are you satisfied with the life of this world rather than the Hereafter? But what is the enjoyment of worldly life compare to the Hereafter except a (very) little." (Quran 9:38)

"Go forth, whether light or heavy, and strive with your wealth and your lives in the cause of Allah. That is better for you, if you only knew." (Quran 9:41)

"Fight those who do not believe in Allah or in the Last Day and who do not consider unlawful what Allah and his messenger have made unlawful and who do not adopt the religion of truth from those who were given the scripture (Christians and Jews) - (fight) until they give the Jizyah (Tax paid by non-Muslim citizens) willingly while they are humbled." (Quran 9:29)

"O prophet, fight against the unbelievers and the hypocrites and be harsh upon them. And their refuge is Hell, and wretched is the destination." (Quran 9:73)

6.2 *Violence in the Hadith*

The Hadith is considered the most trusted and authentic Islamic text next to the Quran itself. An analysis of the text indicates that 97 percent of the references to violence in the Bukhari Hadith refer to warlike violence against non-Muslims. Only 3 percent refer to inward spiritual struggle. The Hadith is also known as 'Sunna' customs. Here are some of the beliefs from the Hadith regarding violence:

"Mohammed once was asked: what is the best deed for the Muslim next

118

to believing in Allah and His Apostle? His answer was: "To participate in Jihad in Allah's cause." (Al Bukhari 1:25)

"Mohammed also said, "The person who participates in Allah's cause and nothing compels him to do so except belief in Allah and His Apostle, will be recompensed by Allah either with a reward or booty (if he survives) or will be admitted to paradise (if he is killed)." (Al Bukhari 1:35)

Narrated by Anas bin Malik: *"Allah's Apostle said, "I have been ordered to fight the people till they say: "None has the right to be worshiped but Allah. And if they say so, pray like our prayers, face our Qibla and slaughter as we slaughter, then their blood and property will be sacred to us and we will not interfere with them except legally and their reckoning will be with Allah."* (Al Bukhari 1:387)

"Mohammed also said, "Know that paradise is under the shades of the swords." (Al Bukhari 4:73)

"Mohammed said, "I have been ordered to fight with the people till they say, none has the right to be worshiped but Allah." (Al Bukhari 4:196)

"Mohammed said to the Jews, "The earth belongs to Allah and His Apostle, and I want to expel you from this land (the Arabian Peninsula), so, if anyone owns property, he is permitted to sell it." (Al Bukhari 4:393)

"Mohammed's last words were: "Turn the pagans (Non-Muslims) out of the Arabian Peninsula." (Al Bukhari 5:716)

Narrated by Abdullah: *"Allah's messenger said, "the blood of a Muslim who confesses that none has the right to be worshiped but Allah and that I am His messenger, cannot be shed except in three cases: in Qisas (equality in the punishment) for murder, a married person who commits illegal sexual intercourse and the one who reverts from Islam (apostate) and leaves the Muslims."* (Al Bukhari 9:17)

Narrated by Ali: *"During the last days there will appear some young foolish people who will say the best words but their faith will not go beyond their throats (i.e., they will have no faith) and will go out from (leave) their religion as an arrow goes out of the game. So, wherever you find them, kill them, for whoever kills them shall have reward on the Day of Resurrection."* (Al Bukhari 9:64)

"Mohammed said No Muslim should be killed... but kill a Kafir (infidel)." (Al Bukhari 9:50)

"Mohammed said, "Whoever changes his Islamic religion, kill him." (Al Bukhari 9:57)

6.3 *What does the Bible says about violence?*

Let me give you a brief comparison of what the Bible says about violence. The biblical teachings are completely contrary to the Quranic and Hadith teachings.

"But to you who are listening I say: love your enemies, do well to those who hate you, bless those who curse you, pray for those who mistreat you. If someone slaps on one cheek, turn to them the other also. If someone takes your coat, do not withhold your shirt from them. Give to everyone who asks you, and if anyone takes what belongs to you, do not demand it back." (Luke 6:27-30)

"Do not gloat when your enemy falls; when they stumble, do not let your heart rejoice." (Proverbs 24:17)

"If your enemy is hungry, give him food to eat; if he is thirsty, give him water to drink. In doing this, you will heap burning coals on his head,

and the LORD will reward you." (Proverbs 25:21, Romans 12:20)

"You have heard that it was said, 'love your neighbour and hate your enemy.' But I tell you, love your enemies and pray for those who persecute you." (Matthew 5:43-44)

"Do not repay evil or insult with insult. On the contrary, repay evil with blessing, because to this you were called so that you may inherit a blessing." (1 Peter 3:9)

"And as you wish that others would do to you, do so to them." (Luke 6:31)

"This is my commandment, that you love one another as I have loved you." (John 15:12)

"So whatever you wish that others would do to you, do also to them, for this is the Law and the Prophets." (Matthew 7:12)

"If anyone says, "I love God," and hate his brother, he is a liar; for he who does not love his brother whom he has seen cannot love God whom he has not seen. And those commandments we have from him: whoever loves God must also love his brother." (1 John 4:20-21)

"You have heard that it was said to those of old, you shall not murder; and whoever murders will be liable to judgement. But I say to you that everyone who is angry with his brother will be liable to judgement; whoever insults his brother will be liable to the council; and whoever says, "You fool!" will be liable to the fire of hell." (Matthew 5:21-22)

CHAPTER 7

Is Muhammad a prophet of God?

There are so many reasons to reject Muhammad as a prophet. I want to tell you that there is no comparison between light and darkness. Please remember that when you talk to Muslim do not compare Jesus with Muhammad, but here I want to give you some comparisons for your knowledge so that you can discern who is from God and who is from the kingdom of darkness.

Muhammad is not the son of God.
The relationship between Muhammad and Allah was one of a slave to his master, with obedience, rather than love.

Narrated by Umar: *"I heard the prophet saying, "Do not exaggerate in praising me as the Christians praised the Son of Mary, for I am only a slave. So, call me the slave of Allah and his apostle."*
(Sahih Bukhari, Volume 4, Book 55, Number 654)

Allah is indeed a master and he can be a kind and forgiving master but he cannot deliver the good as a God of mercy and love.
Jesus is the Son of God. (Luke 3:22)

Muhammad said: *"Allah hates those who don't accept Islam."*
(Qur'an 30:4, 3:32, 22:38)
Jesus said: God loves everyone. (John 3:16)

Muhammad said: *"I have been commanded to fight against people till they testify that there is no god but Allah, and that Muhammad is the messenger of Allah."* (Sahih Muslim 1:33)
Jesus said: *"He who lives by the sword will die by the sword."* (Matthew 26:52)

Muhammad stoned women for adultery. (Sahih Muslim 4206)
Jesus said: *"Let he who is without sin cast the first stone."* (John 8:7)

Muhammad permitted stealing from unbelievers. (Bukhan 44:668, Ibn Ishaq 764)
Jesus said: *"You shall not steal."* (Matthew 19:18)

Muhammad permitted lying. (Sahih Muslim 6303, Bukhari 49:857)
Jesus said: *"You shall not bear false witness."* (Matthew 19:18)

Muhammad owned and traded slaves. (Sahih Muslim 3901)
Jesus neither owned nor traded slaves.

Muhammad murdered those who insulted him. (Bukhari 56:369, 4:241)
Jesus preached forgiveness and forgave those who killed Him. (Luke 23:34)

Muhammad said: *"If then anyone transgresses the prohibition against you, transgress you likewise against him."* (Qur'an 2:194)
Jesus said: *"If someone strikes you on the right cheek, turn to him the other also."* (Matthew 5:39)

Muhammad said: *"Jihad in the way of Allah elevates one's position in Paradise by a hundred fold."* (Sahih Muslim 4645)
Jesus said: *"Blessed are the peacemakers, for they will be called sons of God."* (Matthew 5:9)

Muhammad married 13 wives and kept sex slaves. (Bukhari 5:268, Qur'an 33:50)
Jesus was never married.

Muhammad had sex with a 9 year old child. (Sahih Muslim 3309, Bukhari 58:236)
Jesus did not have sex with anyone.

Muhammad ordered the murder of women. (Ibn Ishaq 819, 995)
Jesus never harmed a woman, He loved and cared for them.

Muhammad said: *"O you who believe! Fight those of the unbelievers who are near to you and let them find in you hardness."* (Qur'an 3:110)
Jesus said: *"Blessed are the meek, for they shall inherit the Earth."* (Matthew 5:5)

Muhammad ordered 65 military campaigns and raids in his last 10 years. (Ibn Ishaq)
Jesus ordered no military campaigns, nor offered any approval of war or violence.

Muhammad killed captives taken in battle. (Ibn Ishaq 451), Muhammad beheaded 800 Jews in a single day. (Sahih Muslim 4390)
Jesus never took captives; never killed anyone.

Muhammad encouraged his men to rape enslaved women. (Abu Dawud 2150, Qur'an 4:24)
Jesus never encouraged rape; never enslaved women.

Muhammad was never tortured, but tortured others. (Sahih Muslim 4131, Ibn Ishaq 436, 595, 734, 764)
Jesus suffered torture, but never tortured anyone. (Isaiah 53)

Muhammad said: *"And fight them until there is no more persecution and religion is only for Allah."* (Qur'an 8:39).

Jesus said: *"Love your enemies and pray for those who persecute you."* (Matthew 5:44)

Muhammad ordered a slave to build the very pulpit from which he preached Islam. (Bukhari 47:743)

Jesus washed His disciple's feet. (John 13:5)

Muhammad demanded the protection of armed bodyguards, even in a house of worship. (Qur'an 4:102)

Jesus chastised anyone attempting to defend Him with force. (John 18:10-12).

Muhammad advocated crucifying others. (Qur'an 5:33, Muslim 16:4131)

Jesus was crucified Himself, and forgave those who killed Him. (Luke 23:34).

According to his followers, **Muhammad** had others give their lives for him. (Sahih Muslim 4413)

Jesus gave His life for others and their sins. (John 18:11 & Isaiah 53)

Muhammad tried to commit suicide many times.

"But after a few days Waraqa died and the divine inspiration was also paused for a while and the prophet became so sad as we have heard that he intended several times to throw himself from the top of high mountains and every time he went up the top of a mountain in order to throw himself down, Gabriel would appear before him and say, "O Muhammad! You are indeed Allah's apostle in truth" whereupon his heart would become quiet and he would calm down and would return home." (Sahih Bukhari, Volume 9, Hadith number 111)

7.1 *The death of Muhammad*

Many Muslims don't know how their prophet died.

"A Jewess brought a poisoned (cooked) sheep for the prophet who ate from it. She was brought to the prophet and was asked, "shall we kill her?" He said "no." Anas added: "I continued to see the effect of the poison on the plate of the mouth of Allah's messenger."
(SAHIH-AL-BUKHARI 2617)

"A Jewess came to Allah's messenger with poisoned mutton and he took of what had been brought to him. (When the effect of this poison was felt by him) he called for her and asked her about that, whereupon she said: I had determined to kill you. There upon he said: Allah will never give you the power to do it. Muhammad said that Allah will never give you power to kill me but this poison killed him because he didn't know Allah well." (SAHIH MUSLIM 5430)

Why did this woman want to kill Muhammad?
"The apostle of Allah sent for Zaynab Bint Al-Harith and said to her: what induced you to do what you have done? She replied: you have done to my people what you have done. You have killed my father, my uncle and my husband, so I said to myself: if you are a prophet the foreleg will inform you; and others have said: if you are a king, we will get rid of you." (IBN SA'D)

The woman killed Muhammad because he killed her people, father, uncle and husband. The Bible says you will reap whatsoever you sow. Jesus said to Peter, *"those who live by the sword will die by the sword."*

"The prophet in his ailment in which he died used to say, "O Aishah! I

still feel the pain caused by the food I ate at Khaibar, and at this time, I feel as if my aorta is being cut from that poison."
(SAHIH AL BUKHARI 4428)

"A Jewess presented (Muhammad) at Khaibar a roasted sheep which she had poisoned. The apostle of Allah ate of it and the people also ate. He then said; lift your hands (from eating) for it has informed me that it is poisoned. Bishrb Al Barab Murural Ansari died. So he (prophet) sent for the Jewess (and said to her): what motivated you to do the work you have done? She said, if you were a prophet, it would not harm you; but if you were a king, I would rid the people of you. The apostle of Allah then ordered regarding her and she was killed. He then said about the pain of which he died: I continue to feel pain from the morsel which I had eaten at Khaibar. This is the time when it has cut off my aorta."
(SUNAN ABU DAWUD 4498)

"The apostle of Allah took the foreleg, a piece of which he put into his mouth. Bishr IBN al Bara took another bone and put it into his mouth. When the apostle of Allah ate one morsel of it Bishr ate his and other people also ate from it. Then the apostle of Allah said: hold back your hands! Because this foreleg has informed me that it is poisoned. Thereupon Bishr said: by him who has made you great! I discovered it from the morsel I took. Nothing prevented me from spitting it out, but the idea that didn't like to make your food unresisting. When you had eaten what was in your mouth, I didn't like to save my life after yours and I also thought you would not have eaten it if there was something wrong. Bishr did not rise from his seat but his colour changed to a green cloth."
(IBN SA'D 252-253)

Muhammad's companion Bishr died from eating the poison. Before he died he told Muhammad that as soon as he took the first bite he could taste the poison. He ate because Muhammad was eating it. Bishr died because he trusted Muhammad.

"Aishah said, "I never saw anyone suffer more pain than the messenger of Allah." (SUNAN IBN MAJAH 1622)

According to Aishah, Muhammad died in great pain.

Here are some reasons that reject Muhammad as a prophet regarding his death.

1. The Quran says that if I am a false prophet Allah will cut my Aorta. (Sura 69)

2. Muhammad had no common sense, he had killed a Jewish woman's family and she offered to cook a meal for them and they accepted it.

3. A Jewish woman gave poison to Muhammad to prove that if you are a true prophet then this poison will not harm you. If you are a false prophet then you will die. He failed the test and died.

4. Muhammad's companion Bishr could taste the poison as soon as he put the lamb into his mouth. Why did he keep eating it? Reason being, he believed in Muhammad? He thought that if there is poison in the food then surely the prophet of Allah will know. Bishr's faith in Muhammad killed him. If he could not keep even simple faith for his dinner then how could he keep faith for his salvation?

5. When Zeenab told Muhammad that she has poisoned him, Muhammad said to her that Allah will not allow him to die with this poison but Allah did allow him to die. If his statement is not true then how can I believe his other statements about salvation?

6. When Muhammad tasted the lamb, the food cried out to him

that it is full of poison. The question remains, why did the lamb not tell him 5 minutes before he tasted it? Or, why do you need revelation after tasting food?

7. The Quran says that when the Jews wanted to kill Jesus, Allah took him to heaven and protected him from death. The question remains - Why Allah protected Jesus but not Muhammad? Allah cared for Jesus but not for Muhammad.

8. Muhammad's daughter, Fatima, asked him when he was on his deathbed will you save me on the day of judgement? Muhammad said to her that he cannot save her. She will be saved by her good deeds. If a man cannot save his own children then how can he save you and me?

9. Allah gave Muhammad whatever he asked and he wanted to marry Aishah, an 8 years old child, Allah granted him his desire; he wanted to have more than seven wives and Allah granted him this request; he wanted to marry his daughter in law, (his adopted son's wife), and Allah approved this. But Allah didn't give him his greatest heart's desire which was to be martyred in a war.

"The prophet said, "By him in whose hands my soul is! I would love to be martyred in Allah's cause and then come back to life and then get martyred and then come back to life and then get martyred and then come back to life again and then get martyred."
(SAHIH-AL-BUKHARI 2797)

CHAPTER 8
Practical Guidelines

I want to give you some practical guidelines to always keep in mind when you meet with your Muslim friends:

- Make friendship with them. Invite them to your home and show hospitality. Let them know that you will serve them halal food. If they invite you, go to their home and eat whatever they offer you.
- Appreciate their food and even ask for the recipe or tell the wife to teach you how to cook the meal you enjoyed the most.
- Dress modestly when you visit their home. Let them feel that you are interested in knowing them as individuals. First win their hearts and then minds.
- Muslims love to be prayed for, so offer your prayers to them. Ask them if you can lay your hands upon them, they will love it. Focus on their problems and pray accordingly. Do keep it short and simple.

A short testimony:
"A couple visited our church, when we lived in Pakistan. They were Muslims. One of our congregants prayed for them. However,

the language she used horrified them, the prayer is understandable for Christians but not for Muslims. The woman prayed that Jesus would cover them with His blood. In Islam, if someone goes to a Muslim priest, the priest will pray over the water and they will then drink it. The Muslim couple came with the same mentality; they bought water with them. The woman also prayed that Jesus would turn the water into His blood. They were appalled as they did not want to drink blood. After that they told the community that Christian people drink blood.

- Do not hesitate to pray for the food because they know that Christians bless their food before they eat it.

- When you visit their home, share your personal experience with God. Especially your personal testimony, how you received Christ. How your life was before receiving Christ and how Christ changed your life and what your life is now after receiving Christ. Talk about the peace which God has given to you or the purpose of your life and the close relationship which you have now with God.

- Show them that you are truthful with your friendship and be sensitive with them with kindness and patience.

- Be knowledgeable regarding Islam. You need to know at least the basics of the Islam. But if you show them that you know aspects of their faith by using their terminology and the Quran, then they will be willing to listen and to welcome you time after time until either you win them to Christ or depart as a friend. The average Muslim does not know the Quran. This will help you to have a strategy which will get you closer to your friend's heart and make you more effective in winning Muslims for Christ.

- When you visit them in their home, take the gospel according to John as a gift for them. It is very easy to read and understood mostly by Muslims. Most Muslims have never read or seen a Bible. So start with the gospel according to John with them. When they finish reading then give them a New Testament. Do not give them the whole Bible in the beginning as they will be bored and will want to give up.

- When they come to your home, show respect for the Bible. Do not place it on the floor or in the bathroom. Muslims still consider it the Word of God, even if they have not read it.

- Muslims are generally superstitious, dealing with witchcraft, fortune telling and charms to protect themselves from evil spirits. They are very fearful people. You need to surround yourself with much prayer. It is advisable to work with intercessors so that you will be covered with prayer before and after witnessing. Always pray afterward to then brush yourself off.

What is a prayer brush off? Here is one model that you can use:

"Thank you heavenly father, for giving me an opportunity to share my faith with this Muslim person. On the basis of my position as a child of God and a joint heir with Christ who has all authority in heaven and on earth, I command every Islamic spirit to leave me and I brush it off from my body, spirit and soul. I wash and cover myself with the blood of Jesus Christ and please, I ask you to bless me, double whatever I have given out today. In Jesus' mighty name. Amen."

- Finally, don't forget your helper the Holy Spirit and your friend Jesus, along the road will give you more fruit and more spiritual sons and daughters.

—